THE
SECOND
WORLD
WAR

A MISCELLANY

NORMAN   FERGUSON

summersdale

THE SECOND WORLD WAR

Copyright © Norman Ferguson, 2014

Illustrations © Shutterstock

Summersdale Publishers Ltd
46 West Street
Chichester
West Sussex
PO19 1RP
UK

www.summersdale.com

Printed and bound in the Czech Republic

ISBN: 978-1-84953-550-2

Substantial discounts on bulk quantities of Summersdale books are available to corporations, professional associations and other organisations. For details contact Nicky Douglas by telephone: +44 (0) 1243 756902, fax: +44 (0) 1243 786300 or email: nicky@summersdale.com.

Dedicated to Private D. N. Traill,
325/71st (Fourth) Heavy Anti-Aircraft
Regiment, Royal Artillery

Contents

Introduction..7

Maps: Major Battles and Important Locations of the Second World War...8

Timeline..11

Allied and Axis Powers...................................19

Pre-war...25

1939..28

The Phoney War..38

1940..43

1941..68

1942..99

1943...127

1944...159

1945...202

Post-war...226

The War in Facts and Figures...........................232

Bibliography...250

Introduction

The Second World War was the bloodiest conflict the world has ever seen. Its beginnings saw a form of warfare developed from that seen in the first global conflict and ended with one whose power would have been unimaginable to those who fought only a few decades before.

It was fought in deserts, jungles, seas, and on mountains and plains, and those affected by it had their worlds turned upside down. This book attempts to tell the story, in a concise but informative way, of those caught up in this complex and brutal war.

Author's note

The story of the war is told in chronological chapters, but some events from different years have been kept together for the sake of the narrative.

Major battles and important locations of the Second World War

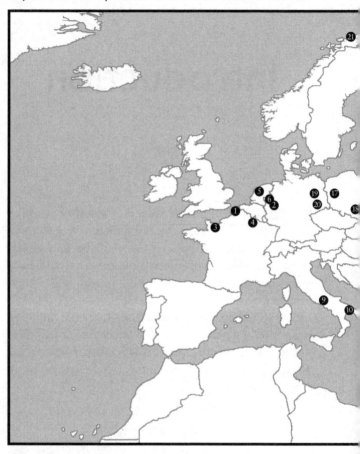

- ❶ Dunkirk
- ❷ Ruhr Dams raid
- ❸ Normandy beaches
- ❹ Ardennes
- ❺ Arnhem
- ❻ Rhine crossing
- ❼ El Alamein
- ❽ Tobruk
- ❾ Monte Cassino
- ❿ Taranto
- ⓫ Stalingrad
- ⓬ Leningrad

⓭ Moscow

⓮ Kursk

⓯ Kiev

⓰ Warsaw

⓱ Oder River

⓲ Auschwitz

⓳ Berlin

⓴ Dresden

㉑ Tirpitz sinking (Håkøy near Tromsø)

The Pacific

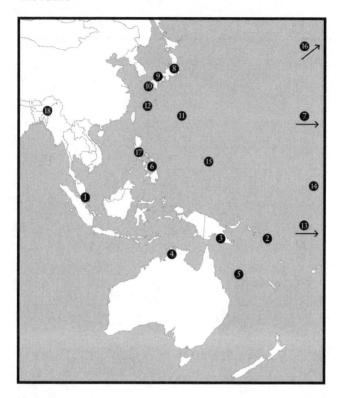

1. Singapore
2. Guadalcanal
3. Port Moresby (New Guinea)
4. Darwin (Australia)
5. Coral Sea
6. Leyte Gulf
7. Midway
8. Tokyo
9. Hiroshima
10. Nagasaki
11. Iwo Jima
12. Okinawa
13. Gilbert Islands
14. Marshall Islands
15. Marianas
16. Aleutian Islands
17. Manila
18. Kohima (Burma)

Timeline

1933

JANUARY

30   Adolf Hitler becomes German Chancellor.

1936

JULY

17   Spanish Civil War begins. Germany and Italy support General Franco's Nationalists.

OCTOBER

25   Germany and Italy sign Rome–Berlin Axis.

NOVEMBER

25   Japan and Germany sign Anti-Comintern Pact. (Italy joins in 1937.)

1937

JULY

7   The Second Sino-Japanese War begins between Japan and China.

1938

MARCH

13   Austria is annexed into Germany in the *Anschluss*.

SEPTEMBER

29–30   Munich Conference takes place, ratifying Germany's annexation of the Czech Sudetenland.

1939

MARCH

15   Germany invades Czechoslovakia.

MAY

22   Germany and Italy sign Pact of Steel.

AUGUST

23   Germany and the Soviet Union sign a non-aggression pact.

SEPTEMBER

1   German forces invade Poland.
3   Britain and France declare war on Germany.
17   Soviet forces invade eastern Poland.

OCTOBER

28   First German aircraft is shot down on UK mainland.

NOVEMBER

30   Soviet Union attacks Finland in what becomes known as the Winter War.

DECEMBER

17   The German pocket battleship *Admiral Graf Spee* is scuttled in Montevideo.

1940

MARCH

16   James Isbister on Orkney is the first British civilian to be killed by enemy bombing.

APRIL

9   Germany invades Denmark and Norway.

MAY

10   German forces attack the Netherlands, Luxembourg, Belgium and France; Winston Churchill becomes Prime Minister of Britain.

15   Dutch army surrenders.

JUNE

4   Dunkirk is captured.

10   Italy declares war on Britain and France.

22   France surrenders.

AUGUST

24–25   Central London is bombed for the first time.

25–26   RAF bombs Berlin for the first time.

SEPTEMBER

7   The Blitz begins.

NOVEMBER

11   Britain attacks Italian fleet at Taranto.

1941

APRIL

6   Axis forces invade Greece and Yugoslavia.

MAY

20   German paratroopers land on Crete.

24   HMS *Hood* is sunk by German battleship *Bismarck*.

27   *Bismarck* is sunk.

JUNE

22   Germany invades Soviet Union.

DECEMBER

7   Japan attacks Pearl Harbor in Hawaii.

1942

FEBRUARY

15   British and Commonwealth troops surrender
          at Singapore to the Japanese.
19   Australian city of Darwin is bombed by
          Japanese.

APRIL

18   US bombers attack Tokyo for the first time.

MAY

7   Battle of Coral Sea begins.

JUNE

4   Battle of Midway begins.

JULY

4   US bombers carry out their first raid in
          northern Europe.

AUGUST

23   Battle of Stalingrad begins.

OCTOBER

23   Second Battle of El Alamein begins.

NOVEMBER

8   Allied forces land in Morocco and Algeria.

1943

JANUARY

31   Germans surrender at Stalingrad.

MAY

16–17   RAF attack Ruhr dams.

JULY

5   Battle of Kursk begins.
10   Allies invade Sicily.

SEPTEMBER

8   Allies announce Italian surrender.

1944

JUNE

6   Allies land in Normandy on D-Day.

JULY

20   Hitler survives assassination attempt.

AUGUST

15   Allies invade south of France.
25   Paris is liberated.

SEPTEMBER

17   Operation Market Garden begins.

OCTOBER

23   Battle of Leyte Gulf begins.

NOVEMBER

12   *Tirpitz* capsizes after RAF raid.

1945

MARCH

24   Rhine is crossed in operation Plunder.

APRIL

13   Soviet troops capture Vienna.
28   Mussolini is killed by Italian partisans.
30   Adolf Hitler commits suicide.

MAY

7   Germany surrenders.

August

6	Hiroshima falls victim to the first atomic bomb.
8	Soviet Union declares war on Japan.
9	Nagasaki is targeted with the second atomic bomb.

September

2	Japan officially surrenders.

Allied and Axis Powers

The belligerent countries in the war formed part of wider alliances. The actions of the Allies were more coordinated than the Axis nations.

AXIS POWERS

Germany – Italy – Japan – Romania – Bulgaria – Hungary

MAIN ALLIED POWERS

Britain – USA – Soviet Union – China – France – India – Canada – Australia – New Zealand – South Africa

THE LEADERS

Name	Nationality	Position
Winston Churchill	British	Prime Minister
Adolf Hitler	German (Austrian-born)	Führer
Franklin D. Roosevelt	American	President
Joseph Stalin	Russian	Leader of Soviet Union
Charles de Gaulle	French	Leader of the Free French movement
Benito Mussolini	Italian	Prime Minister

Year of birth	Year of death	Note
1874	1965	Churchill had commanded a battalion for a short period in the First World War.
1889	1945	Hitler was awarded the Iron Cross in the First World War.
1882	1945	Roosevelt had suffered from polio and attempted to hide his disability from the public.
1879	1953	Stalin was born Josef Vissarionovich Djugashvili but adopted the pseudonym Stalin ('man of steel').
1890	1970	De Gaulle commanded French tanks against the German invasion in 1940 before escaping to Britain.
1883	1945	Mussolini was executed by Italian partisans and his body hung upside down from the roof of a petrol station.

The Commanders

Marshal Georgy Zhukov (Soviet Union)

A conscripted First World War soldier who went on to become a Marshal of the USSR, Zhukov played a vital role in the defence of Leningrad, Moscow and Stalingrad. His strategic genius was put to great effect in the Red Army's offensive in 1944 and 1945, successfully pushing the Germans back.

Air Vice-Marshal Arthur 'Bomber' Harris (Britain)

Harris resisted efforts by Allied commanders to divert bombers away from what he regarded as the main priority of Bomber Command: the heavy bombing of Germany. He believed throughout the war that only an aerial offensive could bring about a collapse in German morale and an end to the conflict.

Air Chief Marshal Hugh Dowding (Britain)

Known as 'Stuffy' for his detached manner, Dowding remained in the RAF after the First World War and at the start of the Second World War was head of Fighter Command. His steady guidance during the critical days of summer 1940 was ill rewarded, as he was removed from his position soon after. He is buried in Westminster Abbey.

FIELD MARSHAL ERWIN ROMMEL (GERMANY)

Hitler described Rommel as 'the most daring commander of armoured forces in the whole of the German army'. In the Battle of France he commanded a panzer division, and was given command of the Axis forces in the Desert War where his exploits earned him the name 'the Desert Fox'. Beaten in the Desert and North African campaigns, Rommel was given command of the Atlantic Wall defences. Suspected of involvement in the plot to assassinate Hitler, he killed himself as his family would otherwise have been targeted by the German security forces. Whether Rommel was part of the plot or not remains unknown.

FIELD MARSHAL BERNARD MONTGOMERY (BRITAIN)

Although tactless and egocentric, 'Monty' as he is universally known, was popular with the soldiers he led and the British public. He was not shy of generating publicity for his generalship, but, despite the unattractive elements of his personality, Montgomery was a successful war commander: he was in charge of the Allied forces that defeated the Germans in northern France in 1944 and his victory at El Alamein was a major triumph at an important point in the war.

GENERAL DWIGHT D. EISENHOWER (USA)

Despite his lack of combat experience, Eisenhower was a perfect choice to be Supreme Commander of the Allied forces in north-west Europe. His calm patience and desire to find consensus allowed him to cope with the differing demands of his competing generals.

FLEET ADMIRAL ISOROKU YAMAMOTO (JAPAN)

Yamamoto realised the value of naval air power and was the originator of the plan to attack the American fleet at Pearl Harbor. Yamamoto had been against war with America, knowing that if it lasted, Japan would be defeated.

Pre-war

Germany needs peace and desires peace.
Adolf Hitler, 1935

THIRD REICH

Once Adolf Hitler gained power in 1933 he instigated a programme of military rearmament, which, although against the terms of the Treaty of Versailles of 1919, helped Germany's economy to recover following the Great Depression. Hitler's tightening of control over Germany allowed him the freedom to determine domestic and foreign policy. In the 'Third Reich' (Third Empire) Germany would seek to expand its territory beyond its borders and persecute those perceived as internal enemies, such as the Jews.

MUNICH CONFERENCE

How horrible, fantastic, incredible it is that we should be digging trenches and trying on gas-masks here because of a quarrel in a faraway country between people of whom we know nothing.

Neville Chamberlain, 27 September 1938. While this was taking place, defences were being built in Britain and the population prepared for possible conflict.

In 1938 Hitler's plans to annexe the Sudetenland, an area inside Czechoslovakia with a predominantly German population, created a crisis when German troops gathered at the border. In late September, representatives from Britain, France, Germany and Italy met in Munich and it was agreed that the Sudetenland would become part of Germany, as long as there were no further territorial aggressive moves. British Prime Minister Neville Chamberlain secured Hitler's signature on a piece of paper on which the Führer promised that Germany and Britain would 'never go to war with one another again'.

On his return to Britain, Chamberlain was greeted with enthusiastic celebrations at having averted war – he appeared on the balcony of Buckingham Palace with the King and Queen – but many, including Winston Churchill, believed it was only a postponement.

I believe it is peace for our time.
Neville Chamberlain, 30 September 1938

TERRITORIAL EXPANSION

Before the war Germany annexed or occupied the following territories:

1936 – Rhineland
1938 – Austria
1938 – Sudetenland
1939 – Czechoslovakia
1939 – Memel/Klaipėda Region (Lithuania)

1939

I am speaking to you from the Cabinet Room at 10 Downing Street. This morning the British ambassador in Berlin handed the German government a final note stating that, unless we heard from them by eleven o'clock that they were prepared at once to withdraw their troops from Poland, a state of war would exist between us. I have to tell you now that no such undertaking has been received, and that consequently this country is at war with Germany.

Neville Chamberlain, radio broadcast, 11.15 a.m.,
3 September 1939

POLAND

In early 1939, another crisis arose as Hitler turned his attention to Poland. In an effort to halt this aggressive move, Britain promised support to guarantee Polish independence. Hitler did not want to provoke war with

Britain, France and the Soviet Union, and in August a non-aggression pact was signed between Germany and the Soviet Union. This paved the way for the Polish invasion and the inevitable war that would result.

DECEPTIONS OF THE WAR: GLEIWITZ

On 31 August Germany stated that Polish troops had attacked a German radio station near the German–Polish border, and were shot by German troops. Although dead Polish soldiers were found, it was part of a ruse: SS soldiers had dressed concentration camp prisoners in Polish army uniforms and shot them to provide a reason for the German invasion.

BLITZKRIEG

On 1 September, 52 German army divisions launched their attack in the first use of 'blitzkrieg' tactics. This form of warfare saw aircraft, tanks, artillery and troops concentrated in rapid assaults to achieve breakthroughs in their opponent's defences. The Polish ground forces were initially overrun and their air force destroyed on the ground, but the Poles were still able to fight a fierce defensive action. On 17 September the Soviet Union invaded the east of the country and a week later Warsaw surrendered. The two aggressors divided up the conquered nation.

Divided Poland (square miles)

Germany – 73,000
Soviet Union – 77,000

694,000

Number of Polish troops taken prisoner by German forces in the 1939 invasion. Around 200,000 were killed or wounded. German losses came to around 44,000.

531

Number of Polish towns and villages burnt to the ground by German troops who also carried out atrocities such as raping women and publicly humiliating Jewish men.

Einsatzgruppen

In the wake of the advance, members of the *Einsatzgruppen* (mobile killing squads) carried out mass executions of Polish civilians. Over 16,000 members of the Polish elite, such as university staff, aristocrats, priests and Jews, were lined up and shot.

British Home Front

Evacuation

As war began, bombing was expected immediately and sections of the civilian population were evacuated from cities expected to be targets. Not everyone went – more than half those eligible refused to go: parents were reluctant to send their children to stay with strangers. Over half of those who left returned home when the feared air raids didn't take place immediately.

Numbers evacuated

Children – 827,000
Mothers with children aged under five – 524,000
Teachers and helpers – 100,000
Pregnant women – 13,000
Disabled persons – 7,000
Total – 1,471,000

Endangered species

For the first time in the history of the zoo we have no poisonous animals here.
Spokesman for London Zoo, 2 September 1939

All poisonous snakes and insects were destroyed and valuable animals such as zebras, Ba-Bar the baby elephant, giant pandas and four chimpanzees (out of the eight who took part in the daily tea party) were transported to other zoos. The zoo remained open.

400,000

Number of pets put down by the RSPCA in London in the first week of the war in order to save food.

BLACKOUT

Blackout regulations were in force by the start of the war, under the emergency lighting regulations, which meant no interior lights were to be visible outside. Offenders could go to prison for up to three months and pay a £100 fine. Vehicle headlights had to be masked and street lighting was switched off.

Put that light out!
Commonly heard exhortation by air-raid wardens.

4,133

Number killed between September and December 1939 in road accidents – double that for the same period the previous year.

The Mayor of Willesden was injured when his car and an ARP ambulance came into collision in Salisbury Road on Tuesday night. He was taken to Willesden General Hospital where he was stated to be comfortable. Five others were hurt.
The Times, 29 August 1940

300,000

Number of people charged with blackout offences in 1940.

44 MILLION

Number of gas masks issued. Britain was the only country to equip its entire population. Babies under two years old were placed inside a respirator that encompassed their whole body, while children aged two to five were given 'Mickey Mouse' masks, so named because of their resemblance to the cartoon character. As it turned out, no gas attacks were made in the war.

RATIONING

Rationing had been carried out in the First World War and was reintroduced, with petrol being rationed in September 1939, food in January 1940 and then clothing in June the following year. An adult in 1942 was given 60 clothing coupons, which were to last a year. Certain clothing items were allocated as per below:

Item details	Vouchers required		
	Man	Woman	Child
Mackintosh, raincoat, cape (except cycling cape), cloak. Fully lined	18	18	11

As above, unlined	9	9	7
Jacket, blouse-type jacket, sleeved waistcoat, coat blazer, cycling cape, woman's half-length cape, woman's bolero. Lined	13	12	8
Sweater, jersey, jumper, pullover, cardigan, woman's bed jacket	8	8	5
Cotton football jersey	4	-	2
Trousers, slacks, over-trousers, breeches, jodhpurs. Lined	11	-	8
Skirt	-	6	4
Kilt	16	14	8
Cassock (woollen)	8	8	7
Undergarments – combinations, petticoat, slip or like garment (woollen)	7	6	4
Corsets	3	3	2

DIG FOR VICTORY

With food scarce, home-grown produce was encouraged. Allotments almost doubled in number to 1.4 million.

PLANKTON

In the face of potential food shortages, scientists considered providing plankton for human consumption. Although rich in fat, proteins and vitamin A, it was too difficult to harvest successfully.

114,000

Number of wartime prosecutions for black-market crimes. The war saw a rise in crime of over 50 per cent, with looters and burglars helped by the darkness of the blackout, and spivs selling contraband goods.

19

Number of times Walter Handy claimed to have been 'bombed out' of his home in five months. Victims were paid compensation for the loss of their home, and with so many houses lost and officials unable to devote time to verifying every case, the system was open to fraudulent claims. Handy was jailed.

PICCADILLY COMMANDOS

Name given to prostitutes who operated in central London. The rise in the number of enlisted men in the capital saw a corresponding increase in female sex workers.

1.5 MILLION

Number of unemployed workers in 1939. The demands of the war economy ensured almost full employment by 1945, with those registered unemployed falling to 54,000.

214

Number of women jailed for refusing to carry out war work.

LORD HAW-HAW

Lord Haw-Haw was the nickname given to William Joyce, an Irish-American Nazi supporter who broadcast propaganda from Germany. Seven million people in Britain tuned in to his radio shows, in which he taunted his listeners. At the war's end he was put on trial and hanged as a traitor by the Allies.

NON-COMBATANT CORPS

Around 6,000 conscientious objectors spent the war carrying out construction and labouring jobs, although some worked at disarming unexploded bombs.

CONSCRIPTION

Conscription began in April 1939 when single men aged between 20 and 22 were called up for six months' service in the armed forces. At the start of the war, the criteria was expanded to all men aged between 18 and 41, and in December 1941 the upper age was raised to 51.

Troops in British Army

| September 1939 | 897,000 |
| June 1940 | 1,656,000 |

Reserved occupations

In 1939 a list of reserved occupations was issued to prevent industrial production being affected by skilled workers leaving their employment, as had occurred in the First World War. The occupations included:

accountant – ambulance driver – architect – bank clerk – basketmaker – blacksmith – bricklayer – cabinetmaker – candlemaker – cartographer – chemist – civil servant – clockmaker – coastguard – coppersmith – crane driver – dentist – docker – doctor – engineer – farm worker – fish-hook maker – fisherman – gardener – glazier – gunsmith – jeweller – joiner – laundry worker – lighthouse keeper – mason – meteorologist – miner – optician – poultryman – prison warder – railway worker – riveter – salesman – saxophone maker – scissors maker – steeplejack – surveyor – tailor – teacher – toolmaker – trade union official – train driver – upholsterer – vet

The Phoney War

After the invasion of Poland, the war settled into a period of relative calm. France and Britain had a numerical advantage over Germany but there were no attempts at mounting a major offensive. Germany's best troops were in Poland and its western border with France was not heavily defended. French troops did make advances but the opportunity to strike further into Germany was not taken. From September 1939 until May 1940 the war was given these terms:

'Phoney War'	USA
'Bore War'	Britain
'Twilight War'	Britain (Winston Churchill)
Sitzkrieg ('Sitting War')	Germany
La Drôle de Guerre ('Funny War')	France

Forces (divisions*) on French–German border (September 1939)

German 23
French 108

(*Soldiers in a division numbered around 15,000–20,000)

160,000

Number of soldiers in the British Expeditionary Force (BEF) sent to France in September. The number reached almost 400,000 over the winter.

First losses

With the war only hours old, German U-boat *U-30* launched torpedoes at the SS *Athenia*, a liner en route to Canada from Glasgow. The resulting 118 civilian deaths – including 28 Americans – caused outrage. U-boats had been forbidden from attacking civilian ships unless they were pre-warned, but the commander claimed it was a Royal Navy cruiser. The mistake was a propaganda coup for the British who were able to highlight the similarities with the sinking of the *Lusitania* in the First World War.

834

Number of sailors who died on the Royal Navy battleship HMS *Royal Oak* on 14 October 1939, from the ship's complement of 1,146. German U-boat *U-47* was able to make its way into Orkney's Scapa Flow from where it launched torpedoes and escaped undetected. Among those lost were 120 sailors aged between 14 and 18.

First casualty

On 9 December 1939, Corporal Thomas W. Priday was part of a patrol in eastern France when he was killed by a booby trap, laid by his own side. He was the first British Army casualty.

268

Number of British ships sunk by German U-boats, mines and ships between September 1939 and May 1940.

*The day will come for total settlement with Hitler
and his gang. Whose side will you be on? Shall
your fathers, sons, brothers, who are already in
Hitler's pay in foreign countries, shall the whole
German people suffer for this? Remember:
he who sows hatred – will reap revenge!*

Text of propaganda leaflet dropped on Germany.
Around 65 million were dropped by the
RAF in the early stages of the war.

THE BATTLE OF THE RIVER PLATE

*I alone bear the responsibility for scuttling the
panzerschiff Admiral Graf Spee. I am happy to pay
with my life to prevent any possible reflection on the
honour of the flag.*
Captain Hans Langsdorff, 20 December 1939

With these words, Langsdorff wrapped himself in the
German navy flag and shot himself. His ship, the pocket
battleship *Admiral Graf Spee*, had been scuttled three
days previously after taking shelter in the Uruguayan
port of Montevideo following its involvement in the
Battle of the River Plate with three British warships.
Thinking there were more Royal Navy ships waiting
at sea than there actually were, Langsdorff ordered his
ship to be put out of action.

WINTER WAR

In order to gain territory, the Soviet Union invaded Finland on the last day of November, in what became known as the Winter War. The Soviets had overwhelming superiority in numbers but their anticipated easy victory was not forthcoming as the Finns fought tenaciously. The Finns were eventually overpowered by the larger Soviet forces and in March 1940 Finland signed a peace treaty.

MOLOTOV COCKTAIL

Finnish troops used improvised anti-tank weapons using glass bottles filled with petrol, lit by a cloth fuse. These were given the name 'Molotov cocktails' after the Soviet Foreign Minister.

505

Number of Soviet troops shot and killed by the 'White Death' – Finnish sniper Simo Häyhä – the most deadly sniper ever.

WINTER WAR LOSSES (DEATHS)

Soviet	200,000
Finnish	25,000

1940

Invasion of Norway

The Navy's here!

Member of the Royal Navy boarding party on rescuing
British prisoners from the German ship *Altmark* in
Norwegian waters on 16 February 1940.

The Phoney War ended with the Germans combining
sea, air and land forces to occupy Denmark and invade
Norway on 9 April, the latter to ensure its supplies of
iron ore from Sweden were maintained. At Norway,
British commanders were surprised, believing the
Germans would not risk coming up against the strong
Royal Navy. French and British forces intervened and
German ships were sunk but the Luftwaffe was able
to support German troops and the Allied forces were
evacuated by mid-June.

NORWEGIAN TOWNS CAPTURED ON THE FIRST DAY OF THE INVASION

Bergen – Kristiansand – Narvik – Stavanger – Trondheim

KÖNIGSBERG

This German warship was the first major naval vessel in warfare to be sunk by aircraft, after being attacked by Fleet Air Arm Blackburn Skuas. Naval losses reduced Germany's ability to support any future invasion of Britain.

ALLIED EXPEDITIONARY FORCES

Name	Objective	Landing site
Rupertforce	Narvik	Harstad
Mauriceforce	Trondheim	Namsos
Sickleforce	Trondheim	Åndalsnes

Mauriceforce was commanded by General Adrian Carton de Wiart, a former First World War soldier who had been awarded the Victoria Cross at the Somme and who had been wounded 11 times in his military career, losing his left eye and left hand.

QUISLING

Following the defeat and occupation by Germany, the name of the Norwegian politician Vidkun Quisling became synonymous with being a traitorous collaborator. In the 1930s Quisling had established the

Norwegian fascist party and following the German invasion was installed as the country's Prime Minister.

PRIME MINISTER CHURCHILL

Winston Churchill was the main cabinet proponent of the Norway campaign but its failure did not cost him his position as First Lord of the Admiralty (as another amphibious assault at Gallipoli had in the First World War). When Neville Chamberlain resigned, Churchill became Prime Minister on 10 May 1940.

FALL GELB

10 MAY 1940

Fall Gelb ('Case Yellow') was the German code name for invasion of the Low Countries and France.

PRE-INVASION FORCES

	Germany	France/Britain/ Belgium/Netherlands combined
Divisions	135	151
Men	2.7 million	3.7 million

THE ATTACK

On 10 May the Germans launched their western offensive, attacking the Netherlands, Belgium, Luxembourg and France. The French and British moved their troops into

Belgium to meet the threat; however, they had been deceived. The German plan was to trick the Allies into thinking this was the main attack: the main drive was in the south, through the thick forests of the Ardennes, an area the French had regarded as impossible for an advance of armoured forces. If the Allies had met them there it could have severely hampered the offensive, but despite evidence of the German build-up they did not change their plans.

FORT EBEN-EMAEL

Regarded at the time to be the strongest fort in the world, this Belgian defensive position was reached by German paratroopers in the early hours of the first day of the invasion. The Germans landed by gliders in the first use of such transportation in warfare. The Belgians were taken completely by surprise and the garrison surrendered the following day. Fighting continued in the rest of the country until Belgium surrendered on 28 May.

850

Number of civilians killed in the Rotterdam Blitz, the bombing of the city by German aircraft on 14 May 1940. The raid on the Dutch city was a mistake, as surrender negotiations were taking place and signals sent to the Luftwaffe bombers to cancel the attack weren't seen. The Netherlands surrendered the same day.

500,000

Number of French soldiers stationed in the Maginot Line. This line of forts, connected by underground chambers, was built in the 1930s. Intended to hold any German advance, the line was 87 miles long but only ran along the border with Germany and stopped short of the Ardennes.

50

Number of airfields in France attacked on the first day of the campaign by German aircraft.

SICHELSCHNITT ('SICKLE CUT')

Term used to describe the German thrust out of the Ardennes intended to cut off the Allied armies.

CROSSING THE MEUSE

German tanks and troops advanced through the Ardennes and reached the important River Meuse. Bridges were destroyed to slow their progress but troops crossed by rubber dinghies, and on 13 May temporary bridges were built to allow vehicles and tanks to cross. The French and British forces were spread thinly and didn't move quickly enough, partly because the roads were clogged with refugees. There was determined resistance in places but once the Germans reached open territory, they were able to move rapidly.

8 MILLION

Estimated number of Belgian, Dutch and French refugees in the summer of 1940.

39

Number of RAF aircraft shot down from 71 that attacked German-held bridges on 14 May. In a raid several days later, only one Blenheim returned from a raid carried out by 12 aircraft.

200 MILES

Distance the Germans advanced in 10 days from the start on the offensive on 10 May. With the Allies expecting to fight a First World War-type war, they were unable to cope with the speed of the German assault.

You are to hold on till dusk. If possible and if any of you are left you may withdraw north east.
Last message received by 2nd Battalion Royal Norfolk Regiment

As the Germans closed in, rear-guard actions were fought, allowing other troops to withdraw. One of these was by the 2nd Battalion Royal Norfolk Regiment, near Le Paradis. After running out of ammunition they surrendered. Ninety-nine of the men were marched to a field and shot or bayonetted to death by Waffen-SS soldiers. Two survived, one of whom was able to testify against the SS unit's commander who was hanged for war crimes in 1949.

DECISIVE EVENTS: DUNKIRK

Nothing but a miracle can save the BEF now.
British General Alan Brooke, II Corps Commander

After crossing the Meuse the German advance had swung north, cutting off British and French troops. They closed in until a pocket of Allied troops was centred on the port of Dunkirk. A counter-attack by British tanks at Arras caused the Germans some concern but their advance continued and the British decided to evacuate.

Royal Navy ships and then civilian boats were called in and more than 330,000 troops were evacuated. Despite the successful evacuation it was a disaster in that huge amounts of material were lost: almost 2,500 artillery weapons and over 60,000 vehicles, material that would be needed to combat a German invasion. It could have been far worse – Churchill had thought only 30,000 men would be brought home. The miracle had been delivered, partly due to a German decision to halt their panzer advance for two days to ready them for future action. It was felt the Luftwaffe would finish off the Allied troops and this pause allowed more men to reach Dunkirk.

TWO-THIRDS

Two-thirds of those rescued were taken from Dunkirk harbour with the rest from the beaches.

845

Number of ships used in the evacuation. The famed 'little ships' were civilian vessels that crossed the Channel to help, but the majority of troops were brought back via navy ships. The small vessels were mainly used to ferry men to the larger ships off shore. Ships that took part included:

barges – destroyers – drifters – corvettes – gunboats – hospital ships – landing craft – minesweepers – motor boats – pleasure boats – punts – RNLI lifeboats – seaplanes – tenders – scoots – torpedo boats – trawlers – tugboats – yachts

MARCHIONESS

One of the 'little ships' was the pleasure boat *Marchioness*. It operated on the Thames until a tragic accident in 1989 in which 51 partygoers died after a collision involving a dredger.

'DUNKIRK SPIRIT'

Description of the attitude that saw a combined and determined effort to bring the soldiers home. Days after the operation the Admiralty issued a statement praising the 'magnificent spirit of cooperation'; the ethos of working together to a common purpose in difficult times is one that still resonates today.

177

Number of RAF aircraft lost. The RAF was criticised by army and navy personnel who felt it wasn't playing its part, but efforts to shoot down enemy bombers before they reached Dunkirk meant they often fought out of sight and squadrons were unable to mount continuous cover from bases in England.

338,226

Allied troops successfully evacuated from Dunkirk between 26 May and 3 June. Over 120,000 were French soldiers, most of whom returned to France shortly after to continue the fighting. Norwegian, Dutch and Belgian soldiers were also taken.

68,710

British Expeditionary Force casualties: killed, wounded or taken prisoner up until the end of the evacuation.

OPERATION ARIEL

Despite the success at Dunkirk, thousands of British Army troops were left behind. More British troops were sent over the Channel following Dunkirk for the Battle of France, but General Sir Alan Brooke soon realised the situation was hopeless and advised a withdrawal. These French

ports – some close to the Spanish border – were
used to evacuate over 190,000 Allied troops:

> Brest
> Cherbourg
> La Pallice
> Nantes
> River Gironde
> Saint-Jean-de-Luz
> Saint-Malo
> Saint-Nazaire

DISASTERS OF THE WAR: *LANCASTRIA*

As Allied troops were being evacuated from
Saint-Nazaire, the troopship *Lancastria* was hit
by German bombers. Around two-thirds of the
estimated 6,000 on board were killed.

Battle for France

Franco–British union

Every citizen of France will enjoy immediately citizenship of Great Britain, every British subject will become a citizen of France.

Part of the radical proposal of 16 June 1940 that advocated Britain and France joining together in a union. The desperate idea was suggested to keep France in the war but was not accepted by the French government.

French surrender

After Dunkirk, the Germans focused on the conquest of France. Paris was taken on 14 June and just over a week later Hitler received the surrender of the French. He arranged for the signing of the armistice to be carried out in the same train carriage as the 1918 armistice document. France had fallen in six weeks.

290,000

French troops killed or wounded in the fall of France.

1,297

Number of French sailors killed on 3 July 1940 by Royal Navy at Mers-el-Kébir in Algeria. The British were concerned that the French fleet would fall into German hands and opened fire, sinking the battleship *Bretagne* and damaging others. The incident showed British resolve to continue the war but deeply affected Franco–British relations.

Vichy France

Following France's surrender, the country was divided into two different sectors: occupied and unoccupied. While German troops were stationed in the northern and western occupied zone, the south was under the jurisdiction of a French government based in the spa town of Vichy, headed by Marshal Philippe Pétain – the hero of the Battle of Verdun in 1916. He led an administration that collaborated with the Nazis. Those regarded as being subversive were arrested and Jews were deported in their tens of thousands to concentration camps.

Following the collaboration between the Vichy French and the Allies in North Africa in November 1942, Hitler ordered the whole of France to be occupied. At the end of the war Vichy leaders were tried for treason by the new French government; Pétain was sentenced to life imprisonment.

Occupied Britain

In June 1940 the Channel Islands became the only part of Britain to be occupied. The islanders faced long years of hardship, and because of the fortifications built by slave labour the islands were bypassed in the D-Day landings and weren't liberated until May 1945.

Defending Britain

We shall go on to the end, we shall fight in France, we shall fight on the seas and oceans, we shall fight with

growing confidence and growing strength in the air, we
shall defend our island, whatever the cost may be, we
shall fight on the beaches, we shall fight on the landing
grounds, we shall fight in the fields and in the streets,
we shall fight in the hills; we shall never surrender.
Winston Churchill, 4 June 1940

250,000

In May 1940, 250,000 British men applied to join the Local Defence Volunteers organisation in 24 hours, following a call for volunteers to combat the threat of invasion by parachutists. By August over 1.6 million had joined what became known as the Home Guard. The organisation comprised men who were not eligible for regular army service due to age, fitness or employment in a reserved occupation. At the beginning the men were without proper weapons and improvised using whatever was to hand:

blunderbusses – carbines – crowbars – elephant guns – flintlock muskets – knives – pickaxes – petrol bombs – chair legs – pitchforks – shotguns – spears – truncheons – hammers – swords – antique revolvers – broom handles – golf clubs

'CROFT'S PIKES'

The Home Guard was issued with around 50,000 bayonets welded to lengths of pipe, which were named after Lord Croft, a War Office minister.

1,200

Over 1,200 Home Guard members were killed on duty during the war.

DEFENCES

Britain rushed to prepare measures to withstand a German invasion. Anti-tank obstacles were built: concrete cubes and 'dragon's teeth' pyramids that could slow or prevent landings by armoured vehicles were constructed along the coast. Poles and girders were placed in fields to stop glider landings and road signs were taken down to confuse invading troops. Oil drums that could be ignited were placed beside roads for use in ambushes.

'CROMWELL'

Code word to signify invasion was taking place. Church bells were also to be rung.

Careless talk

Characters used in the British government campaign to prevent rumour-mongering:

> Miss Leaky Mouth
> Miss Teacup Whisper
> Mr Secrecy Hush-Hush
> Mr Pride in Prophecy

13

The number of children who survived the sinking of the SS *City of Benares*. The ship was taking 90 school children to North America as part of the Children's Overseas Reception Board evacuation programme when on 17 September 1940 it was hit by torpedoes. Some of the survivors spent eight days adrift before being rescued, but many died from exposure. Following the incident the practice of evacuating children and their mothers overseas was abandoned.

> *Wanted Urgently*
> *Scrap Metals*
> *Of All Kinds Excepting Tin.*
> *Place Yours*
> *By The*
> *'Old Gun' Pound Hill.*
> *No rubbish please.*
> Sign for scrap metal collection in Crawley, West Sussex

A drive for scrap metal was started by Lord Beaverbrook, Minister for Aircraft Production. It was claimed to provide metal for munitions and aircraft manufacture but much was dumped. The public got behind the campaign, feeling they were contributing to the war effort. Items collected included:

basins – bandstands – bathtubs – bedsteads – bicycles – bollards – fire irons – gates – kettles – motor cars – pans – ploughs – pots – park railings – scythes – stoves – tramlines – washtubs – watering cans – wheels – First World War tanks

SPITFIRE AND HURRICANE FUNDS

Money was collected in towns, workplaces and donated by rich individuals to 'buy' aircraft for the RAF:

£5,000	fighter
£20,000	bomber

DECISIVE EVENTS: BATTLE OF BRITAIN (10 JULY–31 OCTOBER)

Thank god we're alone now.
Air Chief Marshal Hugh Dowding, June 1940

With France surrendering, Britain faced Germany on its own. In the Battle of Britain the Luftwaffe attempted to prepare the way for invasion. Attacks began on shipping in the English Channel before radar stations and airfields were targeted. The destruction of the RAF was the aim but in early September attention switched to London.

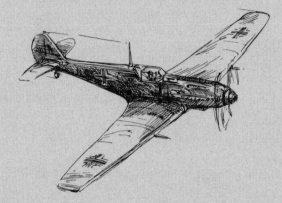

RADAR

Critical to the battle's success was the British use of RADAR (RAdio Direction And Ranging). Developed by scientist Robert Watson-Watt, it allowed the distance and direction of incoming aircraft to be accurately plotted.

Britain's integrated air-defence system (the world's first) centred on Chain Home – a series of radar stations from Britain's south coast to Orkney. German raids were detected at long range

– as they gathered over France – allowing time for RAF fighters to take off and be vectored towards the incoming bombers.

The Luftwaffe bombed the radar masts but failed to pursue these attacks, not realising their importance.

21

Number of Chain Home radar stations along the eastern coastline at the start of the Battle of Britain.

AVAILABLE FIGHTER AIRCRAFT ON 3 AUGUST 1940

RAF	715
Luftwaffe	1,198

AIRCRAFT PRODUCTION TOTALS FOR JUNE 1940

Britain	446
Germany	220

Although outnumbered, Britain's ability to continually resupply its front line squadrons was vital, and stood in contrast to the Germans whose losses were not so readily replaced.

1,253

Number of Fighter Command pilots in mid-July.

OPERATION SEA LION

The German plan was to launch a seaborne invasion along the south coast of England, dependent on air superiority being achieved.

JULIUS CAESAR

Code name of British defensive plan for the German invasion.

2,820

Number of British citizens named in the Gestapo's 'Black Book', which contained a list of those who would be detained upon the invasion of Britain.

ADLERTAG (EAGLE DAY)

The Germans launched their offensive against the RAF on 13 August. Fighter Command lost 13 aircraft to the Germans' 46.

RAF STATIONS ATTACKED BETWEEN 12–18 AUGUST

Andover – Benson – Biggin Hill – Brize Norton – Cardiff – Colerne – Croydon – Detling – Driffield – Eastchurch – Gosport – Harwell – Hawkinge – Hullavington – Kemble – Kenley – Lympne – Manston – Martlesham Heath – Middle Wallop – Sealand – Tangmere – Thorney Island – West Malling

BATTLE OF BRITAIN DAY

The attacks continued through August and into September, and the Luftwaffe mounted what they planned would be a decisive strike on 15 September. They expected to meet weak resistance, but Spitfire and Hurricane squadrons had been replenished and 60 German aircraft were shot down. Following this the Germans abandoned plans for invasion.

10 MINUTES

Length of time German fighters could spend over London due to their limited range.

1,733

German aircraft shot down in the battle.

THE FEW

The RAF's pilots, despite an image of cheerful boyishness, gained a reputation for dogged determination, flying mission after mission while physically and mentally exhausted. These men – who would become known as The Few following a speech by Winston Churchill on 20 August – came from these countries:

Australia – Austria – Barbados – Belgium – Britain – Canada – Czechoslovakia – France – Ireland – Jamaica

– New Zealand – Newfoundland – Poland – Rhodesia
– South Africa – USA

126

Number of enemy aircraft shot down by 303 (Polish) squadrons in six weeks.

'ADOLFS'

Polish fighter pilots' nicknames for German aircraft they shot down.

2,940

Number of Fighter Command airmen who flew in the battle.

537

Number of Fighter Command aircrew killed in the battle.

718

Number of Bomber Command aircrew killed. RAF bombers attacked airfields and ports where invasion barges were concentrated.

*Never in the field of human conflict was so much owed
by so many to so few.*
Winston Churchill, 20 August 1940

THE BLITZ

When some German aircraft mistakenly dropped their bombs on central London on the night of 24 August, it provoked an RAF raid on Berlin. Hitler reacted by ordering British cities to be targeted. The Blitz was about to begin.

On 7 September German bombers attacked London during the day and continued through the night. Four hundred and thirty-six Londoners were killed and 1,600 badly injured. More than 400 died in the following evening's raid, setting the pattern that was to continue until May 1941. It was not easy to shoot down bombers at night but once RAF fighters had been equipped with airborne radar their effectiveness improved: 75 raiders were shot down in April 1941.

6,945

British civilians killed in September 1940; 5,730 of these were in London.

THE BROWN FAMILY

On the first night of the Blitz, Charles Brown lost his wife Norah and their seven children:

Elizabeth Ada (24)   Doris (6)
Charles Thomas (20)   Joan (3)
Edith Violet (11)   Ann (8 months)
Vera (9)

'TRUMPETS OF JERICHO'

High-explosive German bombs designed to emit a loud whistling noise as they fell.

NICKNAMES AND WEIGHTS OF GERMAN BOMBS

Hermann	2,200 lb
Satan	4,000 lb
Max	5,500 lb

51,509

Number of British civilians killed during the war from bombing raids.

3.6 MILLION

Number of Anderson shelters produced. Designed to provide a cheap form of bomb shelter, they were made of corrugated metal and could be enhanced with turf placed on top.

Major towns and cities bombed

Aberdeen – Belfast – Birmingham – Bristol – Cardiff – Clydebank – Coventry – Edinburgh – Falmouth – Glasgow – Hastings – Hull – Leeds – Lincoln – Liverpool – London – Manchester – Newcastle – Nottingham – Plymouth – Portsmouth – Sheffield – Southampton – Swansea

Moonlight Sonata

The German code name for the bombing of Coventry on the night of 14–15 November 1940, which devastated the city and left the famous cathedral in ruins. Thirty-three thousand incendiary bombs were dropped on the city, an important target due to its munitions factories – three-quarters of which were damaged. Over 500 people were killed.

57

Consecutive nights London was bombed in September and October 1940.

8

Number of houses that remained undamaged after two nights of bombing in Clydebank in March 1941. Ten members of one family died in intensive raids that left over half the population homeless.

TREKKING

Name for the practice of those who walked out of towns and cities at night to escape the bombing. Ten thousand people left Southampton each night.

DARING RAIDS: TARANTO (11 NOVEMBER)

Italy joined the war on Germany's side in June 1940. As its fleet was a threat to Allied shipping in the Mediterranean, a force of 21 Royal Navy Fairey Swordfish biplanes attacked the port of Taranto. The Swordfish were slow but capable torpedo carriers. Despite heavy anti-aircraft fire, three Italian battleships were badly damaged, for the loss of two Swordfish. The rest of the Italian fleet moved northwards to Naples and played a minor role in the rest of the war. The Japanese studied the attacks and used their findings a year later at Pearl Harbor.

1941

We must be the great arsenal of democracy.
US President Franklin D. Roosevelt, 29 December 1940

LEND-LEASE ACT

Passed in March 1941, while America was still a neutral nation, Lend-Lease allowed the Allies to receive supplies from the USA. Countries such as Britain (which received around half of all Lend-Lease aid), France, China and the Soviet Union received material such as food, oil, weapons and equipment. The Soviet Union, which started receiving aid after June 1941, received around $11 billion worth in the form of:

> 7,000 tanks
> 11,400 aircraft
> 400,000 jeeps
> 1.75 million tons of food

$270 BILLION

Total value of Lend-Lease assistance received by Britain from America.

WOMEN AT WAR

In December 1941 British women were conscripted for the first time. Single women aged 20 to 30 and widows without children were first in line, but the age range was expanded by 1943 to include women aged 19 to 43. Women under 50 who had served in the First World War could also be called up. They had the choice of war work in factories or on farms, or military service. Women were not permitted to fight but could join women's branches of the armed services in support roles.

MILITARY

WOMEN'S AUXILIARY AIR FORCE (WAAF)

By July 1943, 182,000 women were 'Waafs'. They interviewed returning bomber crews, plotted fighter sorties, interpreted photo reconnaissance images, drove bomb trucks and operated barrage balloons, as well as more mundane clerical and cooking duties. Almost 200 Waafs were killed over the course of the war.

WOMEN'S ROYAL NAVAL SERVICE (WRNS)

'Wrens' performed many duties, from loading torpedoes on to submarines to administrative work. Over 74,000 were in the service by 1943; 303 Wrens were killed in the war.

AUXILIARY TERRITORIAL SERVICE (ATS)

The ATS was the women's branch of the army and women carried out the same duties as the men except from taking part in combat, although in anti-aircraft batteries they did everything bar press the firing button. Over 250,000 served – most of the drivers in the army were women. Twenty-two ATS members became prisoners of war and over 300 died.

CIVILIAN

WOMEN'S LAND ARMY

The Land Army was established to provide enough food for the nation. 'Land Girls' worked on farms where hard manual labour was required. A working week of 48 hours was expected and time off was half a day a week with a week's holiday per year. At its peak in 1943 there were 87,000 members.

TIMBER CORPS

Over 8,000 women volunteered to become 'lumberjills' working in forestry.

WOMEN'S VOLUNTARY SERVICE FOR CIVIL DEFENCE (WVS)

The WVS was Britain's largest organisation employing women. It carried out a wide range of activities that included: helping European refugees, supporting the evacuation of children, providing clothing and food for bombed-out families, and even babysitting. By the summer of 1941, 920,000 were in the WVS.

AIR RAID PRECAUTIONS FOR CIVILIAN DEFENCE (ARP)

Three hundred thousand women served in the ARP services as wardens, ambulance drivers, first-aiders and telephonists.

1.4 MILLION

Number of ARP wardens (both men and women) during the war.

AUXILIARY FIRE SERVICE (AFS)

The AFS provided additional help to regular fire services during air raids and was merged with local fire brigades in 1941 to become the National Fire Service. Fifty thousand women joined, including 2,600 full time. Twenty-five women died in the fire services during the course of the war.

Air Transport Auxiliary (ATA)

The ATA delivered new and repaired aircraft to squadrons. Of the 1,245 volunteer pilots, 168 were women – one of whom was pioneer flyer Amy Johnson who lost her life on a delivery flight in 1941. The ATA delivered over 300,000 aircraft.

'Hitler's Helpers'

Nickname for rats, for their consumption of large quantities of food. One of the tasks carried out by women of the Land Army was to exterminate vermin such as rats, rabbits and moles from farms.

1 in 3

By the end of 1943 a third of British factory workers were women.

90 per cent

By September 1943, 90 per cent of single, able-bodied women were in employment.

2,151,280

Number of women who had registered for essential war work or service in the armed forces by 27 September 1941.

1,700

Distance in miles British and African troops advanced in two months in their offensive against Italian forces in East Africa. The Italians suffered over 300,000 casualties in their attempt to defend their short-lived empire in the area.

ALBERT HORN

The name given by a German pilot captured after his aircraft crashed in Scotland. Horn turned out to be Rudolf Hess, Hitler's deputy, who had flown 900 miles on a solo mission, which he claimed was to make peace with Britain. Hess spent the rest of his life a prisoner in Berlin, dying in Spandau Prison in 1987.

SINKING OF THE *BISMARCK*

The battleship *Bismarck* was the German fleet's flagship. It was commissioned in August 1940 but it wasn't until May 1941 that it left port for operational duties. With the *Prinz Eugen* it sailed north past Norway then through the Denmark Strait between Greenland and Iceland in the north Atlantic. On 24 May *Bismarck* encountered the British battle cruiser HMS *Hood* and battleship HMS *Prince of Wales*. The *Hood* was sunk dramatically when shells hit the ship's magazine and the *Prince of Wales* suffered severe damage. Damaged herself, *Bismarck* sailed south but gave away her position by radioing Germany. Aircraft and ships attacked and *Bismarck* was unable to continue. She was scuttled and sunk on 27 May, with over 2,000 of her crew being lost.

3

Number from HMS *Hood*'s crew who survived from the 1,419 on board.

BALKANS CAMPAIGN

With Mussolini keen to have Italy prove its worth as an ally of Germany, Italian forces invaded Greece in October 1940, launching their attack from Albania. A month later they were pushed back by counter-attacking Greeks who made further gains in January 1941. The Germans came to the aid of their Axis ally and invaded Greece at the start of April 1941. Britain sent troops and aircraft but many commanders had misgivings about the likelihood of success. The Germans had the advantage in equipment and men and, coupled with air supremacy, were unstoppable. The Greeks, British and Commonwealth troops were forced south until Athens was taken at the end of the month. The campaign lasted just over three weeks.

50,732

Number of British, Commonwealth and Greek troops evacuated from Greece.

151

Number of Germans killed in Operation Punishment – the German invasion of Yugoslavia in April 1941. The offensive lasted just 12 days and captured more than 250,000 prisoners of war. Many Yugoslavs joined the guerrilla campaign including Josip Broz, known as Tito, the country's future president.

CRETE

On 20 May German paratroopers landed on Crete in the first ever large-scale airborne invasion. The 35,000 defending Allied troops, who had been evacuated from the Greek mainland, were short of artillery and air cover, and the Germans were able to gain a foothold, securing the airfield at Maleme, allowing reinforcements to be flown in. During the initial landings the German paratroopers suffered heavy losses, with many shot before they reached the ground. A fifth were killed and Germany abandoned launching airborne assaults for the rest of the war. An Allied evacuation was ordered on 27 May.

3 MINUTES

Every three minutes a German Junkers transport aircraft landed at Maleme on the third day of the invasion.

11,370

Number of British and Commonwealth troops captured at Maleme.

DESERT WAR

The Desert War was fought along the strip of coastline of northern Egypt and Libya. Territory was gained and lost as fortunes swung from the Germans and Italians on one side, and the British and Commonwealth on the other. The British were keen to hold on to their territory in Egypt, to retain access to the Suez Canal and nearby oil facilities.

The Italians made the first move, attacking in September 1940. Italy had entered the war as France was about to fall and Mussolini expected Britain to follow soon after. He was keen to secure a notable victory before the war ended and his troops advanced until they reached Egypt. They were counter-attacked by the British Army's Western Desert Force, which pushed the inadequately trained and equipped Italians back. So began the war of reversals.

THE DESERT WAR MAIN ATTACKS

Key
→ Axis advance   ← British advance
(eastwards)   (westwards)

1940

SEPTEMBER ————————————————→

Italians advance and reach Sidi Barrani in Egypt.

←———————————————— DECEMBER

British mount Operation Compass, pushing back Italian forces and leading to a rout in February 1941; 130,000 prisoners of war are taken.

1941

MARCH ————————————————→

Field Marshal Erwin Rommel takes effective command of German and Italian forces, and mounts raids that develop into a major advance that forces the British back to Egypt by May.

← ————————————————————— **NOVEMBER**

British mount Operation Crusader. British forces push Rommel back to El Agheila in Libya.

1942

JANUARY ———————————————————————→

Rommel, now reinforced, attacks. British retreat back to the defensive Gazala Line.

MAY ———————————————————————————→

Rommel circumvents Gazala Line. British withdraw to El Alamein.

JULY ——————————————————————————→

First battle of El Alamein. Stalemate results as British halt German–Italian attack.

← ————————————————————— **OCTOBER**

British, with General Montgomery in charge, succeed in pushing the Germans and Italians back all the way into Tunisia.

Khyber Pass to Hell-Fire Pass

Message chalked on 4th Indian Division lorry. Halfaya Pass was an important part of the route from Egypt to Libya.

242

Duration in days of the siege of Tobruk in 1941. The Libyan port was besieged by superior numbers of Germans and Italians and was relieved as part of Operation Crusader in December 1941. The story of Tobruk was not over and in June 1942 34,000 Allied troops were taken prisoner after a surprise attack by Rommel. Tobruk was retaken by the Allies in November 1942.

Situation shambles.

Message sent as Tobruk was captured in June 1942.

5

Number of times the Libyan city of Benghazi changed hands between 5 February 1941 and November 1942.

'THE DESERT RATS'

The German propagandist Lord Haw-Haw had described those British and Commonwealth troops besieged in Tobruk as being like rats in a trap. The troops then called themselves 'the Rats of Tobruk'. The name was later widened to include all men of the Eighth Army.

TROOP NATIONALITIES IN THE EIGHTH ARMY

Australian	Indian
British	New Zealand
French	Polish
Greek	South African

69 PER CENT

Casualty rate from one regiment of the Royal Horse Artillery in one battle in 1942. Although gunners were normally less at risk than tank crews or infantry, in the Desert War battles were mobile and batteries were more likely to be reached by the enemy.

90 SECONDS

Time one had to escape from an Allied Sherman tank that had caught fire. Shermans gained the nickname 'Ronsons' (from the make of cigarette lighters) for their propensity to catch fire when hit.

SPECIAL AIR SERVICE

The SAS began as a small force of commandos recruited to carry out raids behind enemy lines. In one attack it destroyed 61 German aircraft.

GAZALA GALLOP

The Eighth Army's retreat eastwards in June 1942.

'ASH WEDNESDAY'

British headquarters in Cairo burnt secret documents, in preparation for what seemed like the certain German capture of the city.

THE FLYING CAN OPENERS

Nickname given to the RAF's 6 Squadron for its attacks destroying Axis tanks. Their Hawker Hurricanes were equipped with two 40 mm cannons.

DECISIVE EVENTS: OPERATION BARBAROSSA

We have only to kick in the door and the whole rotten structure will come crashing down.
Adolf Hitler, 1941

The Soviet Union and Germany had signed a non-aggression pact in 1939, but this was cast aside in the summer of 1941 as Hitler ordered a German invasion of the Soviet Union – intended to quickly destroy the Soviet armed forces and force a subsequent surrender.

Although Soviet forces were more numerous Hitler gambled on a speedy victory preventing these greater resources being deployed. The German high command had been encouraged by the Soviets' poor showing against the much smaller Finnish army in the Winter War, and their confidence seemed well placed: the German forces initially made huge gains, driving forwards as much as 30 or 40 miles a day.

The attack was the biggest military operation ever mounted, taking place across a wide front, from the Black Sea to the Baltic. Despite large losses, the Red Army was not wiped out, and fresh reinforcements were available from a massive conscription programme that would see over 30 million men called up for service in the Red Army.

LEBENSRAUM

Hitler envisaged western Soviet territories as providing *lebensraum* – 'living space' – which Germans could colonise. The resident Soviets would be sent eastwards, or kept for slave labour.

1,080

Length in miles of the initial front. As the Germans advanced, it widened to 1,800 miles.

GERMAN ARMY FORMATION AND OBJECTIVES

Army Group North → Baltic states, Leningrad

Army Group Centre → Moscow

Army Group South → Ukraine, Caucasus

3,517

German panzers taking part in the initial offensive. There were twice as many artillery guns.

625,000

Number of horses used by the Germans. Despite the mechanised nature of warfare, much of the transportation was carried out by horses.

3.6 MILLION

Axis troops taking part in the initial attacks. They were mostly German but also from Bulgaria, Finland, Hungary, Italy, Romania and Slovakia.

4.5 MILLION

Number of Soviet troops opposing the offensive.

4,000

Number of Soviet air force aircraft lost in the first five days. Most were destroyed on the ground.

747,870

Soviet casualties in the first two weeks.

213,301

German casualties in the first six weeks.

370

Distance in miles the German Army Group Centre advanced in three weeks.

It is probably no overstatement to say that the Russian campaign has been won in the space of two weeks.
German General Franz Halder, 3 July 1941

STRATEGY

As the Germans moved deeper into Soviet territory Hitler made what could be regarded as the most important decision of the whole war, in ordering the main thrust of his forces to Moscow, and aiming for Leningrad in the north and the Ukraine in the south. Kiev was taken in mid-September following a successful encirclement but by the time Hitler ordered his forces to concentrate on Moscow, the chance to take the Soviet capital was lost.

ENCIRCLEMENTS

The wide-open spaces of the Soviet interior were ideal for mobile warfare. With it came the risk of envelopment and the Soviets experienced great losses as the Germans encircled their armies.

Date (1941)	Location	POWs taken
June	Minsk	300,000
July	Smolensk	300,000
August	Uman	107,000
September	Kiev	437,000
October	Moscow (Vyazma and Bryansk)	688,000

2,593

Number of Soviet factories moved east in the face of the German advance. The Soviet ability to maintain production of munitions and equipment proved vital.

BABI YAR

Over 33,000 Ukrainian Jewish men, women and children were machine-gunned by German troops in three days at the end of September in a ravine near Kiev called Babi Yar. It began a series of executions there that would see an estimated 100,000 civilians and prisoners of war killed.

We have underestimated the Soviet colossus.
German General Franz Halder, 11 August 1941

OPERATION TYPHOON

The delayed offensive to take Moscow began on 2 October. The Germans made strong gains – one panzer unit so surprised the city of Orel that trams were still operating as their tanks rolled in. A 300-mile-wide breach was made in the Soviet front to the west of Moscow but the Germans failed to take advantage. Panic in Moscow ensued and the government packed up to move east – even Lenin's tomb was transported out – but Stalin decided to remain in the city and the mood changed to resilience. Defences were built and troop reinforcements were brought in.

The autumn weather played a part, turning the roads into a quagmire, slowing the German troops whose tanks were not as mobile in the mud. When the frosts came, the roads hardened and became suitable for the German tanks to move.

The Soviets fought hard, causing the Germans in November to consider whether to continue. They carried on, and pushed the Red Army back but with men and materials becoming exhausted, the offensive ground to a halt. The inadequately clothed and equipped Germans suffered in the freezing cold. The Soviets had brought in troops suited to winter combat from Siberia and in early December the Red Army counter-attacked, forcing the Germans to retreat. Moscow was saved.

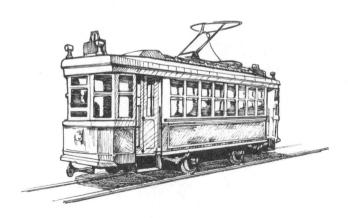

440,000

Number of Moscow citizens mobilised to build the city's defences.

9

Miles from Moscow the Germans reached. Reconnaissance patrols could see the golden spires of the Kremlin.

720 MILES

Distance the Germans advanced into the Soviet Union.

RASPUTITSA

Russian 'rainy season' – which began in October.

−35 °C

Temperature reached on 4 December. Vehicle engines wouldn't start and soldiers suffered from frostbite.

30

Number of survivors of 44th Mongolian Cavalry Division who charged at Klin, outside Moscow in November. Two thousand began the horse-mounted charge across an open field. No Germans were killed or injured.

> *Strike the enemy day and night.*
> Red Army General Georgy Zhukov's directive
> to troops, 9 December 1941.

150 MILES

Distance German units were pushed back in 10 days as Zhukov's troops continued their counteroffensive.

918,000

German casualties by end of January 1942 since the beginning of Barbarossa.

4.8 MILLION

Soviet casualties from the start of Barbarossa to the end of December 1941.

4 MILLION

Number of Soviet troops by December 1941. With the original Red Army almost wiped out, it depended on fresh recruits and, although inexperienced, they were able to mount effective counter-attacks.

'ORDER OF THE FROZEN MEAT'

German nickname for campaign medal awarded to those who endured the winter of 1941–42.

'STALIN ORGANS'

German nickname for Soviet Katyusha multi-barrelled rocket launchers.

Siege of Leningrad

The Führer has decided to erase the city of Petersburg [Leningrad] from the face of the earth. We have no interest in the preservation of even a part of the population of that city.

German army Directive No 1a 1601/41, 22 September 1941.

The Germans were unwilling to risk high losses in capturing Leningrad after cutting it off in the summer of 1941. They opted to bomb and starve it into submission. There was widespread hardship: citizens were reduced to eating rats – and even their fellow citizens – while being under heavy artillery and aerial bombardment. Eventually supplies were transported via the 'Road of Life' over the frozen Lake Ladoga. The citizens held out until being relieved in January 1944 by Soviet forces.

886

Number in Leningrad arrested in winter 1941–42 for cannibalism.

Boots

To acquire their boots soldiers would hack the legs off dead troops, and hang them over a fire until they thawed.

890 days

Duration of siege.

1.5 MILLION

Estimated number of citizens who died from disease, enemy attack and starvation.

CONFERENCES

Conferences were held at which the major Allied leaders met to discuss strategy and take some of the most important decisions of the war.

Date	Location	Participants	Code name
9–12 August 1941	Placentia Bay, Newfoundland	Churchill, Roosevelt	Riviera
22 December 1941–14 January 1942	Washington DC	Churchill, Roosevelt	Arcadia
21–25 June 1942	Washington DC	Churchill, Roosevelt	-
12–17 August 1942	Moscow	Churchill, Stalin	Bracelet
14–24 January 1943	Casablanca	Churchill, Roosevelt	Symbol
11–25 May 1943	Washington DC	Churchill, Roosevelt	Trident
17–24 August 1943	Quebec	Churchill, Roosevelt	Quadrant
23–26 November 1943	Cairo	Churchill, Roosevelt	Sextant

28 November–1 December 1943	Tehran	Churchill, Roosevelt, Stalin	Eureka
3–7 December	Cairo	Churchill, Roosevelt	Sextant
12–16 September 1944	Quebec	Churchill, Roosevelt	Octagon
9–19 October 1944	Moscow	Churchill, Stalin	Tolstoy
30 January–3 February 1945	Malta	Churchill, Roosevelt	Argonaut/Cricket
4–11 February 1945	Yalta	Churchill, Roosevelt, Stalin	Argonaut/Magneto
17 July–2 August 1945	Potsdam	Churchill, Truman, Stalin, Attlee	Terminal

I have said this before, but I shall say it again and again and again; your boys are not going to be sent into any foreign wars.
US President Roosevelt, 1940 election campaign

DECISIVE EVENTS: PEARL HARBOR (7 DECEMBER)

In order to improve its economic position Japan started to acquire territory. Knowing its expansionist moves would bring America into the war, Japan elected to strike a decisive blow to destroy the US Navy. Although the surprise raid was a victory for the Japanese, it wasn't as successful as they would have wished – US aircraft carriers were at sea and undamaged by the raid.

JAPANESE ATTACK FORCE

First wave	Second wave
49 bombers	54 bombers
40 torpedo bombers	–
51 dive bombers	78 dive bombers
43 fighters	36 fighters

Tora! Tora! Tora!

This message, translating as 'Tiger! Tiger! Tiger!', was sent to the Japanese fleet by Captain Mitsuo Fuchida, who had planned the mission and led the first wave. It indicated that the attack had achieved total surprise.

KGU AM

Incoming Japanese aircraft used music being broadcast by this Honolulu radio station as a navigation aid.

B-17s

The incoming Japanese raid was detected but put down to being a flight of American B-17 bombers returning from a training mission.

Air Raid On Pearl Harbor X This Is Not Drill

Telegrammed message sent to navy units on 7 December 1941 by US Navy's Pacific commander.

LOSSES

American	Ships	Japanese
USS *Arizona* USS *California* USS *Maryland* USS *Nevada* USS *Oklahoma* USS *Pennsylvania* USS *Tennessee* USS *West Virginia*	Battleships	–
USS *Helena* USS *Honolulu* USS *Raleigh*	Cruisers	–

USS *Cassin* USS *Downes* USS *Helm* USS *Shaw*	Destroyers	–
USS *Curtiss*	Seaplane tender	–
USS *Utah*	Target ship	–
USS *Vestal*	Repair ship	–
USS *Oglala*	Minelayer	–
USS *Sotoyomo*	Tug	–
–	Midget submarines	5
Floating drydock YFD-2	Ancillary vessels	–

All but three of the ships were recovered and repaired.

2,403

Number of Americans who died in the attack. Over 60 were civilians, many killed by their own side's anti-aircraft shells.

> *Yesterday, December 7, 1941 – a date which will live in infamy – the United States of America was suddenly and deliberately attacked by naval and air forces of the Empire of Japan.*
>
> US President Franklin D. Roosevelt, Joint Session of Congress, 8 December 1941

GREATER EAST ASIA CO-PROSPERITY SPHERE

Title given by Japanese to their programme of expansion that began before the war. Manchuria was occupied in 1932 and other parts of China in the late 1930s. French Indo-China saw 35,000 Japanese troops arriving in July 1941. As it attacked at Pearl Harbor, Japan began further acquisitions. Over the next six months it invaded and occupied the following countries and territories:

Andaman and
Nicobar Islands
Borneo
Burma
Christmas Island
Dutch East Indies
Guam
Hong Kong

Malaya
New Guinea
Philippines
Singapore
Solomon Islands
Thailand
Wake Island

HMS *Prince of Wales* and HMS *Repulse*

Sailing to Singapore on 10 December 1941, these Royal Navy warships were hit by Japanese torpedoes and bombs. They were the first major warships to be sunk from aerial attack at sea.

殺光、燒光、搶光
('Kill all, burn all, destroy all')

This was the 'Three Alls' Japanese policy against the communists in China, ordered in December 1941. This scorched-earth strategy is estimated to have resulted in over 2.5 million Chinese civilian deaths.

The forces fighting against the Japanese in China were split: the Nationalists under Chiang Kai-shek and the Communists under Mao Zedong. They were bitterly opposed to each other and never united to fight the Japanese. The long-running war in China tied down large numbers of Japanese troops.

1942

THE CHANNEL DASH

On 11 February 1942 a German navy battle group that included the cruisers *Scharnhorst*, *Gneisenau* and *Prinz Eugen* left the French port of Brest in Operation Cerberus, which became known as the Channel Dash. They were attempting to reach German home ports and took a risk travelling through the narrow English Channel. Despite Royal Navy and RAF attacks, none of the German warships were sunk.

Daring Raids: Saint-Nazaire (27–28 March)

In an attempt to prevent the German battleship *Tirpitz* from using the dry dock in the French port of Saint-Nazaire, the British mounted a bold operation (later described by its participants as 'the greatest raid of all'). An elderly destroyer, HMS *Campbeltown*, was packed with explosives and deliberately crashed into the harbour gates. It sat until the next day, when a delayed action timer set off the explosives, wrecking the gates: *Tirpitz* was denied its Atlantic base. Of the 621 British navy personnel and commandos who took part over 200 were taken prisoner and 168 were killed.

Burma

In early 1942 the Japanese continued westwards, into Burma. The British-run colony was poorly prepared to resist the offensive – British commanders didn't think the countryside was passable and had a low opinion of the Japanese soldier (something that would soon change) – and by the middle of the year British forces were pushed out of the country into neighbouring India. They made attempts to mount offensives but the Japanese counter-attacked and held them off.

ALLIED FORCES IN BURMA

Indian soldiers and airmen made up the majority of the forces who served in Burma:

Indian	340,000	Chinese	66,000
British	100,000	American	60,000
African	90,000		

60,000

Number of troops in the Indian National Army who fought on the Japanese side.

SITTANG BRIDGE

The bridge at Sittang was blown up by retreating British troops on 23 February 1942 to prevent the Japanese from gaining an easier route to Rangoon. However, this left over half the British forces on the wrong side of the river.

1,000

Distance in miles the British retreated in 1942 towards the Indian border.

THE CHINDITS

Led by Orde Wingate, the Chindits were a special forces unit formed to carry out long-range penetration missions behind enemy lines. (Their name stemmed from the chinthe – a mythical half-lion/half-dragon beast that guarded Burmese temples.) This force of British, Burmese and Nepalese Gurkha soldiers had mixed success but provided a morale boost for the Allies.

DISASTERS OF THE WAR: FALL OF SINGAPORE (FEBRUARY)

The worst disaster and largest capitulation in British history.
Winston Churchill

The British colony of Singapore, at the southern end of the Malayan peninsula, was an important strategic location. It guarded India to the west and Australia to the south. On the same day as they bombed Pearl Harbor, the Japanese landed troops on the Malayan coast. They advanced south, using bicycles to move quickly overland and ships to leapfrog down the coast, reaching Singapore in early February. With low morale and facing a determined enemy, the British-led forces were unable to mount a solid resistance. The surrender on 15 February 1942 was the British Army's biggest ever defeat. It signalled the beginning of the end of Britain's empire in the Far East.

600 MILES

Distance Japanese advanced in 54 days in the capture of Malaya and Singapore.

130,000

Number of British, Australian, Indian and Malay troops taken prisoner.

55,000

Number of Japanese troops who captured Singapore.

BATTLE FOR MALTA

The small Mediterranean island was a vital resupply base for North Africa. Before any planned landings, German and Italian aircraft bombed it with great intensity, starting in June 1940. The bombing was almost continuous and the islanders suffered from malnutrition as supplies ran low. RAF aircraft were flown to help its defence but were constantly outnumbered and at times there were no aircraft available to take off. In March 1942 Spitfires finally arrived. The British used Malta to strike back and supplies for Rommel's desert campaign were affected by aircraft flying from the island. In 1943 German attacks were halted.

154

Number of continuous days and nights of bombing on Malta in 1942.

To honour her brave people I award the George Cross to the island fortress of Malta to bear witness to a heroism and devotion that will long be famous in history.

King George VI, in a letter announcing the awarding of the George Cross to the island, 15 April 1942

BOMBER COMMAND

There are a lot of people who say that bombing can never win a war. Well, my answer to that is that it has never been tried yet, and we shall see.

Air Marshal Arthur 'Bomber' Harris, 3 June 1942

The RAF's Bomber Command provided a means of attacking Germany in the early years of the war. Once the 'Phoney War' was over raids began to take place against key sites, however accuracy was a problem, with crews often unable to find, let alone bomb, their targets. Navigational equipment, crew training and the bombers themselves were gradually improved.

Casualties were high from the outset of the conflict, with the early bombers being shot down by anti-aircraft artillery and fighter aircraft during daylight raids. Bomber crews formed 2 per cent of the British armed forces but suffered 14 per cent of the casualties.

12

The number of Wellington bombers shot down in a daytime raid on German shipping near Heligoland on 18 December 1939. Twenty-four had taken off from Britain. Another three crashed on returning to base and a further three were written off. Daylight raids were subsequently abandoned.

1 IN 5

A government report in August 1941 found that only one in five RAF bombers came within 5 miles of its target.

1,047

Number of RAF bombers taking part in the first '1,000 Bomber Raid' on 30 May 1942. The target was Cologne; 486 Germans were killed and 3,330 buildings destroyed.

CHRISTMAS TREES

German name for target flares dropped by RAF Pathfinder aircraft.

CORKSCREW

Violent evasive manoeuvre practised by RAF bombers to shake off enemy fighters.

1 IN 4

Chances of Bomber Command aircrew surviving their first tour of operations. The rate fell to one in ten in their second tour.

30

Number of operational sorties to be flown by bomber crews in a 'tour'. After two tours they would be removed from the operational list and wouldn't have to fly any more combat missions, although some did volunteer for a third tour.

11 PER CENT

Percentage of German armament production lost in 1944 from Allied bombing.

9 PER CENT

Average yearly loss of German production caused by Allied bombing.

17 PER CENT

Percentage of Bomber Command personnel in 1944 who were women.

'BRYLCREEM BOYS'

Nickname for RAF airmen who were regarded as being more glamorous than their compatriots in the other services.

WINDOW

Code name for strips of aluminium dropped by RAF bombers as they approached enemy territory. The metal confused German air defence radars.

KAMMHUBER LINE

Named after the colonel in the Luftwaffe who devised it, the German air defence system consisted of an integrated network utilising radar, searchlights and night fighters, designed to strike at Allied bombers. It ran from Switzerland to Denmark.

KORFU

The German Korfu detection equipment was so effective it could pick up British H2S bombing radar transmissions while the bombers were still on the ground at their bases.

SCHRÄGE MUSIK

German night fighters were equipped with upward-firing cannons that allowed them to fire accurately into the undersides of the bombers' fuselages. The name for this weapon system came from the German word *schräg* which means 'sloped', relating to the angle of the guns.

95

Number of aircraft lost on the night of 30 March 1944 in a raid on Nuremberg, from the 795 that took part in what was Bomber Command's costliest mission. German night fighters were able to wreak havoc on the bombers, which caused little damage to their intended target. Five hundred and forty-five RAF aircrew were killed.

Baedeker Raids

Bath – Canterbury – Exeter – Norwich – York

These five historic British cities were targeted in the spring and summer of 1942. It was claimed they were picked from a Baedeker travel guidebook, as retaliation for the RAF bombing of the picturesque German town of Lübeck.

Lidiče

In May 1942 Czech resistance fighters assassinated Reinhard Heydrich, SS Deputy Reichsprotektor of Bohemia and Moravia in Czechoslovakia. In retaliation, Hitler ordered the killing of all adult males in villages connected to those responsible for Heydrich's death. In the village of Lidiče, 173 men were executed, almost 200 women were sent to Ravensbrück concentration camp, and 100 children were sent from the village. A small number of the children were given to German families while others were gassed in specially equipped vans. Seventeen of the children were eventually returned to their families after the war.

Special Operations Executive (SOE)

And now set Europe ablaze.
Winston Churchill, on SOE's formation

The SOE was established to carry out sabotage and subversion operations behind enemy lines. Known as the Baker Street Irregulars because of the location of their headquarters, the operatives were trained in all aspects of covert warfare. In operations bridges were blown up, trains derailed and – in one of its greatest successes – a Norwegian heavy water plant in Telemark that was to be used in the production of Germany's atomic weapons was destroyed. By the summer of 1944, there were 13,000 members of SOE, 3,000 of whom were women.

43

Number of SOE agents out of 57 sent to occupied France between June 1942 and autumn 1943 who were caught by the Germans. Thirty-six were executed.

DISASTERS OF THE WAR: DIEPPE (19 AUGUST)

This raid on the French port of Dieppe was intended to test German defences. Along a 10-mile front, 5,000 men from the Canadian 2nd Infantry Division were landed along with 1,000 British commandos. The Germans were prepared and casualties were high. Some success was achieved, but overall it was a failure and served as a lesson for future amphibious landings.

83 PER CENT

Casualty rate for Royal Regiment of Canada.

DARING RAIDS: THE DOOLITTLE RAID (18 APRIL)

In the wake of Pearl Harbor, US commanders decided a strike against Japan would provide a morale boost. Led by Lieutenant Colonel James Doolittle, 16 B-25 Mitchell medium bombers took off from the USS *Hornet* aircraft carrier and achieved total surprise in the first air raid on Japan. It was impossible for these medium bombers to land back on the aircraft carrier and plans were made for them to fly on to China, but none were able to make it to their intended landing sites. One aircraft flew to the Soviet Union where the crew were interned. The rest of the aircraft made it to China where they ditched in the sea, made forced landings or crashed following the crews baling out. Eight crewmen were captured by the Japanese: three were executed and one died in prison, and the remaining four were freed in 1945. The Japanese took revenge on the Chinese civilian population who had aided the downed flyers and an estimated 250,000 were killed.

Bataan Death March

Japanese forces began their invasion of the Philippines in December 1941. The Americans and Filipino troops retreated to the Bataan peninsula. They held out for four months, hoping for reinforcements, but on 9 April 1942, starving and ill, they surrendered. Around 75,000 were taken prisoner. Forced to march to a prison camp 65 miles away, they were denied food and water, beaten and bayonetted. An estimated 10,000 died. Arriving at the camp saw no end to the callous treatment and 400 were dying each day. Only a third of the captured US troops and half the Filipinos survived the war.

I shall return.

US General Douglas MacArthur, on arriving in Australia in March 1942 following his forced departure from the Philippines.

'The Yangtze Rapids'

US Marine name for dysentery.

Battle of the Coral Sea

This naval battle, fought between the US and Japanese navies south-east of New Guinea on 7–8 May 1942, was the first in the history of warfare where opposing ships didn't see each other: the engagement was carried out by aircraft. Aircraft carriers from both sides were sunk: the Japanese lost the light aircraft carrier *Shoho* and the Americans the USS *Lexington*. For the first time the Japanese had been stopped in the Pacific and their plans to capture Port Moresby in New Guinea, which would allow them to strike at nearby Australia, were stalled.

DECISIVE EVENTS: MIDWAY (4–7 JUNE)

The battle of Midway doomed Japan.
Captain Mitsuo Fuchida, senior air commander, Japanese fleet

The Japanese were embarrassed by the Doolittle Raid and resolved to destroy the US carriers to prevent it recurring. Led by Admiral Yamamoto, who had commanded the Pearl Harbor raid, the Japanese sailed towards the mid-Pacific US base at Midway Island.

The US Navy was in possession of intelligence provided by codebreaking of Japanese signals that guided their actions while the Japanese were unaware of the close proximity of American aircraft carriers. Japanese intelligence had discovered an American task force was at sea, but the message wasn't passed on because of strict radio silence policy.

While Japanese fighters were preoccupied at sea level with attacking US torpedo bombers, three squadrons of Dauntless dive bombers began their own bombing runs. Three Japanese carriers were set on fire within minutes. The battle continued but eventually both sides withdrew. The Americans, which had lost their carrier USS *Yorktown*, had won a notable victory, which prevented further Japanese expansion towards Fiji, New Caledonia and Samoa.

7

Number of US torpedo bombers that returned from an attacking force of 51. From one squadron, VT-8, only one aircrew member survived: Ensign George H. Gay.

8 MINUTES

Within this time three of the four Japanese aircraft carriers were fatally damaged or destroyed by US Navy aircraft. The fourth was hit later.

JAPANESE CARRIERS SUNK AT MIDWAY

Akagi ('Red Castle')
Kaga ('Increased Joy')
Hiryu ('Flying Dragon')
Soryu ('Green Dragon')

337

Number of Japanese aircraft lost, almost half the Japanese carrier-based aircraft.

Papua and New Guinea

With their plans to capture Port Moresby by sea being curtailed, the Japanese attempted an overland route through Papua. In the way was 100 miles of mountainous jungle terrain. They began in July 1942.

Defending the Kokoda Trail south were Australian and American troops. In August the Allies defeated the Japanese at Milne Bay – the first time the Japanese had been beaten in a land battle during the war.

Fighting continued until January 1943 when the Allies took the last of the Japanese positions in the area. Fighting continued in New Guinea through the war.

30 MILES

Distance Japanese got to within Port Moresby.

Cannibalism

There were reports Japanese troops had eaten the flesh of dead Australian prisoners. This provoked revulsion and inspired fighting where little quarter was given. The normal rules of warfare were abandoned; prisoners were seldom taken.

64

The Australian port of Darwin was bombed 64 times by the Japanese. Over 250 people were killed in the first raid in February 1942.

Decisive Events: Guadalcanal (7 August–February)

Six hundred miles east of Papua, Guadalcanal is the largest of the Solomon Islands. To halt the Japanese advance through the southern Pacific, Allied troops – predominantly American – landed in August 1942. The main objective was to capture a partially built Japanese airfield, which they named Henderson Field. The Allies quickly took it then had to defend it. The fighting was carried out in an unwelcoming, hot, humid and disease-ridden location. After months of combat, the Americans finally prevailed in early 1943.

'Tokyo Express'
US nickname for Japanese resupply ships that were forced by US aircraft to operate at night.

'Washing Machine Charlie'
Nickname given to a Japanese bomber, seen over American positions every night, due to the irregular sound of its engines.

24 minutes
Duration of the first engagement of the three-day naval Battle of Guadalcanal, fought in November. In this action the Japanese lost three ships; the Americans lost six.

> **13,000**
>
> Number of troops the Japanese managed to evacuate in February 1943. They had lost around 24,800 casualties; US casualties numbered 7,600.

5TH SS PANZER DIVISION *WIKING* ('VIKING')

A number of volunteers from outside Germany served in the Waffen-SS, the combat arm of the SS. In the 'Wiking' division the following countries were represented in October 1942:

Country	No of volunteers
Belgium	124
Denmark	324
Finland	597
Netherlands	932
Norway	126
Sweden	7
Switzerland	9

Decisive Events: Stalingrad August 1942– February 1943

In the summer of 1942 the Germans were not capable of mounting an offensive across the whole of the Eastern Front as they had the previous year. The objectives were to move south and capture the Caucasus oilfields. Hitler added the taking of Stalingrad, a decision that would prove disastrous.

The Luftwaffe reduced much of the city to rubble but the demolished buildings created an ideal environment for the defenders. The two sides fought a bloody and costly urban battle, and the Germans held nine-tenths of the city, but the Soviets were able to resupply and reinforce across the Volga River. In November the Red Army struck back.

Uranus

On 19 November the Red Army launched a twin-pronged offensive: Operation Uranus, which cut through Romanian troops defending parts of the line and encircled the Sixth Army, which consisted of 250,000 men. Its commander, General Friedrich Paulus, requested permission to break out but Hitler refused, demanding the army stand and fight. Efforts made to relieve them failed. Two months later the starving and frozen army surrendered.

> *Surrender is forbidden. Sixth Army will hold their position to the last man and the last round and by their heroic endurance will make an unforgettable contribution toward the establishment of a defensive front and the salvation of the Western World.*
>
> Adolf Hitler to General Paulus, 24 January 1942

700 TONS

Amount of supplies required each day by the Sixth Army. The Luftwaffe promised Hitler this could be supplied by air but only around 90 tons were delivered daily.

'NIGHT WITCHES'

German nickname for pilots of the Soviet all-women 588th Night Bomber Regiment who attacked their positions in low-level raids. The Soviet Union was the only country to utilise female aircrew in combat.

BOMB DOGS

The Red Army strapped explosives to dogs, which were remotely detonated when the animals neared German tanks.

31 JANUARY

On this day Paulus surrendered. Hitler had promoted him to Field Marshal the day before, knowing that no German of that rank had ever been taken alive and expecting Paulus to kill himself. He was held prisoner until 1953.

> *I have no intention of shooting myself for this Bohemian corporal.*
> Field Marshal Paulus

6,000

The number of German and Romanian prisoners of war who returned home after being captured at Stalingrad. Ninety thousand had been originally taken prisoner.

225

German troops shot by Soviet sniper Vasily Zaytsev at Stalingrad.

13,000

Number of Soviet soldiers at Stalingrad executed for the crimes of desertion or cowardice in the face of the enemy. Tough discipline was a feature of Soviet command methods and armed 'blocking units' would remain behind front-line troops to discourage any slackening of resolve.

1.1 MILLION

Soviet casualties at Stalingrad, of which half were fatalities.

Stalingrad is no longer a town. By day it is an enormous cloud of burning, blinding smoke; it is a vast furnace lit by the reflection of the flames. And when night arrives, one of those scorching, howling, bleeding nights, the dogs plunge into the Volga and swim desperately to gain the other bank. The nights of Stalingrad are a terror for them. Animals flee this hell; the hardest stones cannot bear it for long; only men endure.

Unknown German soldier

THE ICEBERG CARRIER

One of the most unusual ideas of the war was the proposal by scientist Geoffrey Pyke to build aircraft carriers out of ice. A demonstration saw a bullet bouncing off and hitting a senior US navy figure. The project ran out of time and money and was abandoned.

DISASTERS OF THE WAR: PQ17

*Most Immediate. Cruiser force withdraw to
westward at high speed.*
Message from Admiralty, 4 July 1942

As part of the effort to support the Soviet Union's
war effort, the western Allies sent convoys via the
Arctic Ocean. On 27 June 1942 convoy PQ17 left
Icelandic waters with 36 merchant vessels. The
Royal Navy commanders in the Admiralty were
fearful of the German battleship *Tirpitz* being in
the area and ordered the escorting cruisers to leave
the convoy to face any attack by the German ship.
When the destroyers accompanying also turned
away, the merchant vessels were left without any
adequate defence. They were ordered to scatter.
Over the following days German U-boats and
aircraft sank 24 ships, killing 153 merchant
seamen. Arctic convoys were halted until better
methods of protection could be introduced.

DECISIVE EVENTS: EL ALAMEIN
(23 OCTOBER–4 NOVEMBER)

*I am afraid that things are not going our way.
The opposition is too strong and our own force
is worn out.*

Field Marshal Erwin Rommel, in a letter to his wife,
4 July 1942

*Here we will stand and fight; there will be
no further withdrawal.*

General Montgomery, 13 August 1942

After two years of fluctuating fortunes, the British
had been pushed back to El Alamein. It sat between
the Mediterranean Sea to the north and the Qatari
depression – a natural feature inaccessible to tanks
– to the south. General Bernard Montgomery,
recently arrived commander of the Eighth Army,
planned an attack that was to be attritional:
wearing down the enemy before a breakout could
be achieved. Following a strong artillery barrage,
his forces made their way through minefields
before tackling the heavily defended Axis positions.
RAF air power and strong artillery fire eventually
broke down the defences. Hitler ordered Rommel
to stand fast but it wasn't enough against an
opposition gaining the upper hand.

CHURCH BELLS

Church bells were rung in Britain to celebrate, the first time they had done so since Dunkirk in 1940.

DECEPTIONS OF THE WAR: EL ALAMEIN

As the British were building up their forces in the north, decoy supply depots, tanks and other material were left visible to be discovered by German aerial reconnaissance in the south.

'THE DEVIL'S GARDENS'

Around 500,000 mines were laid by the Germans in minefields.

TROOP NUMBERS

British/Commonwealth	195,000
German/Italian	104,000

30,000
Axis prisoners taken at El Alamein.

13,500
British casualties.

This is not the end. It is not even the beginning of the end. But it is, perhaps, the end of the beginning.
Winston Churchill, 9 November 1942

OPERATION TORCH

Churchill insisted the United States assist Britain to defeat Germany before tackling Japan. With the Soviets pressing for a 'Second Front' against Germany – and the Allies not yet capable of invading Europe – North Africa was chosen as the location where those American forces would make their first appearance out of the Pacific theatre.

The invasion that began on 8 November 1942 saw 100,000 US and British troops land in Algeria and Morocco. Some US troops landed directly after their trans-Atlantic crossing. These territories were held by

Vichy French forces who were on the Axis side, but they switched to join the Allies following the landings. As this force moved east into Tunisia, Montgomery's Eighth Army was advancing west from Libya. The campaign was disorganised and mistakes were made by both sides – at the Kasserine Pass the US forces fell into disarray – but in May 1943 the Allies prevailed and Tunis was taken.

238,000

Axis prisoners of war taken by the Allies in the North African campaign.

1943

BEVIN BOYS

Nickname for men conscripted into the coal-mining industry in Britain rather than the armed forces to prevent a shortage of coal: Ernest Bevin was the Minister for Labour and National Service. Around 48,000 Bevin Boys were employed, including the future comedian Eric Morecambe.

GOMORRAH

The destruction was so immense that of many people literally nothing remains. From a soft stratum of ash in a large air raid shelter the number of persons who lost their lives could only be estimated by doctors at 250 to 300.

Report by Hamburg Police President, 1 December 1943

Gomorrah was the code name for a series of missions by RAF Bomber Command against the German city of Hamburg carried out in late July and early August 1943. The use of incendiaries combined with dry weather created a firestorm, with winds reaching 170 miles per hour and temperatures of 800 °C. Smoke reached up to 20,000 feet and around 900,000 Germans were made refugees.

38,975

Total number of German deaths in these raids on Hamburg.

57

Number of German civilians killed in the raid on 2 August in the town of Elmshorn, where they had been evacuated after escaping the Hamburg raids.

EIGHTH AIR FORCE

Aircraft for the United States Army Air Forces (USAAF) began arriving in Britain in July 1942 and started with bombing missions over France before making their first raids on Germany in January 1943. The Americans preferred to fly daylight missions, to improve accuracy, while relying on tightly flown formations for defence, with the bombers' many machine guns forming a protective zone around the formations. Its strength grew and by 1944 the 'Mighty Eighth' could put 2,000 bombers and 1,000 fighters into the air.

THE SCHWEINFURT–REGENSBURG MISSION

On 17 August 1943 the USAAF mounted a raid on two targets: the ball-bearing plant at Schweinfurt and the Messerschmitt fighter factory at Regensburg. Of the 376 bombers that set out 60 were shot down, with German fighters lining up to attack the aircraft whose escort fighters were unable to accompany them for the whole distance of their missions.

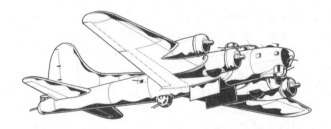

20

Number of missions flown in Europe by American B-24 pilot James Stewart. Stewart resumed his acting career in Hollywood after the war.

409

Number of B-17 Flying Fortress and B-24 Liberator bombers lost in April 1944 – the Eighth Air Force's heaviest month of losses.

426,000

Number of USAAF personnel based in UK by the end of the war.

MUSTANG, THUNDERBOLT AND LIGHTNING

The P-51 Mustang, P-47 Thunderbolt and P-38 Lightning were US fighters given the task of bomber escort. The Mustang was one of the great aircraft of the war, able to fly all the way to Berlin and back from their bases in south-east England.

540 MPH

Maximum speed of the Messerschmitt Me 262, the world's first operational jet aircraft. Fourteen hundred were built but its potential was never realised due to fuel shortages and engine reliability issues.

89

Number of US bombers that flew on to the neutral countries of Sweden or Switzerland in March and April 1944.

50 PER CENT

Loss rate in May 1944 of Luftwaffe fighters – a rate that couldn't be sustained.

INVASION OF SICILY

With North Africa secured, the Allies made their first major landing on Axis-occupied Europe. On 9 July

1943, Allied forces came ashore in Sicily and faced fighting in a landscape that suited the defenders.

DECEPTIONS OF THE WAR: THE MAN WHO NEVER WAS

In Operation Mincemeat British intelligence went to great lengths to fool the Germans and Italians into believing the Sicily landings were only a feint for the main landings to take place in Greece. The body of Glyndwr Michael, a Welsh vagrant who had died after eating rat poison, was dressed in the uniform of a Royal Marines officer, taken by submarine to a position off the coast of Spain where he, along with a briefcase containing false plans, was placed in the water. The Germans fell for the deception. Two weeks after the Sicily landings, Hitler still believed Greece would be the main invasion location.

You can forget about Sicily. We know it's Greece.
General Alfred Jodl, German Armed Forces High Command, on telephone to other German senior officers, May 1943

180,000
Allied troops who landed in Sicily.

12
Total number of gliders out of the force of 144 carrying British airborne troops to Sicily that landed at their designated sites. Strong winds blew British

and American airborne troops widely off course – half ended up in the sea.

CASUALTIES

German/Italian:	169,000
British:	15,564
American:	8,781

110,000

Number of Axis troops who were evacuated to mainland Italy.

ITALIAN CAMPAIGN

The Italian government has surrendered its armed forces unconditionally.
General Dwight D. Eisenhower, 8 September 1943

Following the successful invasion of Sicily, Allied troops landed on the Italian mainland in September. The Italians surrendered just before the landings were made and German forces moved in to face the invaders. At Salerno the Americans were almost forced back into the sea but they held on and after heavy air and naval support, which saw reinforcements being landed, the Germans withdrew northwards. Naples was reached by the Allies at the beginning of October.

Despite Churchill's description of Italy as the 'soft underbelly' of Axis territory, the Allies found progress slow as they fought their way up the mainland. Weather played its part, turning roads into quagmires, and the Germans fought tenaciously, using the defensive advantages of the craggy terrain.

In January 1944, the Allies hoped to steal a march on the Germans by a push from the south at Cassino combining with an amphibious landing north, to force the Germans to withdraw northwards towards Rome.

MONTE CASSINO

This Monastery MUST be destroyed and everyone in it as there is no one in it but Germans!
USAAF 96th Bombardment Group briefing,
15 February 1944

The strategically located Monte Cassino formed a central part of the Gustav defensive line. The monastery was the sixth-century birthplace of the Benedictine order of monks and its bombing by the Allies was controversial. Hundreds of civilian refugees were killed inside. The fighting at Monte Cassino continued for a further three months.

KOBLENZ MEN

A ceasefire was arranged on 14 February so that both sides could retrieve their dead from the battlefield. A German soldier told American Lieutenant Colonel Hal Reese that he remembered seeing American troops in

Koblenz in 1919. Reese produced a photograph of himself in Koblenz – he had been one of those troops.

Anzio

The landing at Anzio on 22 January 1944 started well with very light resistance. However, instead of advancing towards Rome which was 30 miles away, the troops dug in. The Germans, who didn't withdraw as the Allies hoped, vigorously counter-attacked. Pressure was now on the troops at Cassino to break through and relieve the Anzio units – the opposite of the original plan.

Wojtek the Bear

Polish troops played an important role in the battles in Italy, although one of their number stood out from the other soldiers. Wojtek was a brown bear that had been adopted as a mascot by a Polish artillery unit in the Middle East and then properly enlisted in the army in order for him to be shipped to Italy, where he helped move supplies. After the war he spent the rest of his life in Edinburgh Zoo.

'ANZIO ABSCESS'

Hitler's description of the Allied beachhead.

DEFENSIVE LINES

As the Allies advanced the Germans used various defensives lines that ran across Italy:

Albert Line	Dora Line
Arno Line	Gothic Line
Barbara Line	Gustav Line
Bernhardt Line	Hitler Line
Caesar Line	Viktor Line

GUSTAV LINE

In May the Gustav Line was finally breached and Polish troops took the battered remnants of the monastery at Monte Cassino. The Germans began to withdraw and, though the opportunity to cut them off was available to US General Mark Clark, he opted instead to advance on Rome, reaching the city on 4 June. The German troops that withdrew formed part of the forces in Italy that continued fighting until the end of the war.

MARCUS AURELIUS CLARKUS

Nickname for US General Mark Clark by his own staff officers. Clark employed 50 public relations staff.

Eighth Army order of battle

At the beginning of the assault on the Gothic Line as part of Operation Olive on 25 August 1944, the Eighth Army was made up of the following units:

5th Corps

1st Armoured Division (including 43rd Gurkha Lorried Infantry Brigade)
4th Division
46th Division
56th Division
4th Indian Division
1st Army Group Royal Artillery
Corpo Italiano di Liberazione

10th Corps

10th Indian Division
9th Armoured Brigade
2nd Army Group Royal Artillery

1st Canadian Corps

5th Canadian Armoured Division
1st Canadian Division
21st Tank Brigade
1st Canadian Army Group Royal Canadian Artillery

2nd Polish Corps

3rd Carpathian Division
5th Kresowa Division
2nd Polish Armoured Brigade

ARMY RESERVE

2nd New Zealand Division
3rd Greek Mountain Brigade

GURKHAS

The Gurkhas are one of the most well-known group of soldiers in the British armed services. During the war these renowned troops from Nepal were awarded nine Victoria Crosses, and as well as Italy saw action in Burma, Greece and the Desert War.

'D-DAY DODGERS'

Derogatory term for soldiers who fought in the Italian campaign. With the main focus of attention from June 1944 on the north-west European campaign, there was an attitude among some that the fighting was easier in other areas. The troops used it as inspiration for a song to the tune of 'Lili Marlene'. The Italian Campaign continued until May 1945 when German forces surrendered.

CAMPAIGN CASUALTIES

Allied: 312,000
German: 435,000

ULTRA

The enemy knows all our secrets and we know none of his.

Admiral Karl Dönitz, German Navy Commander-in-Chief, 12 November 1943

The Allies possessed a weapon throughout much of the war that remained a closely kept secret for decades after the war had ended. At a compound in Buckinghamshire called Bletchley Park, codebreakers were able to read signals and understand German navy, air force and army intentions. It was called ULTRA due to its secrecy classification: above top secret. As with all secret information-gathering, the Allied commanders battled with how much information they could act upon, thereby risking discovery of their codebreaking successes.

ENIGMA

The German Enigma cipher machines were the first to have their codes broken, initially by the Poles before the start of the war, who passed on their information to Britain. These machines worked using keyboards connected to rotor wheels that could produce millions of possible combinations. Enigma machines were used by many branches of the German military to transmit information.

STATION X
Code name for Bletchley Park. Around 7,000 people worked there at its peak.

'GOLDEN EGGS'
Churchill's name for the revealed secrets.

Bronze goddesses

The electro-mechanical machines, or 'bombes', designed to help find the correct wheel combinations used in German Enigma code machines.

U-110

On 9 May 1941 HMS *Bulldog* captured intact U-boat *U-110*. Crewmen boarded the German submarine and recovered a complete Enigma encryption machine and the German navy code books.

500,000

Number of German navy signals read at Bletchley Park.

Boniface

The name of a fictional MI6 secret agent who the British invented as the source for the intelligence gained by decryption.

Tunny

Tunny was the British code name given to the Lorenz code machines, used by German High Command. The Lorenz machines used 12 wheels offering millions of possible combinations.

ALAN TURING

Turing was a British mathematician who played a vital part in developing computational machines to break Enigma and Lorenz codes. His work laid the foundations for the modern computer. He died in 1954 from cyanide poisoning following his arrest and conviction for homosexuality, which was illegal in Britain at that time. He was pardoned in 2013.

COLOSSUS

The world's first programmable computer, built to break Lorenz codes. It could read 5,000 characters a second. Colossus was designed by Tommy Flowers, an ex-Post Office engineer. At first Lorenz codes were broken by hand but the Colossus and earlier Heath Robinson machines helped speed up the process.

DECISIVE EVENTS: BATTLE OF THE ATLANTIC

The Battle of the Atlantic was one of the most crucial conflicts of the entire war. Britain's very survival depended on supplies of food, munitions, raw materials and fuel being shipped from North America and other parts of the world. The battle had begun on the first day of the war with the sinking of the SS *Athenia* by a U-boat. German surface raider ships and long-range Focke-Wulf Condor aircraft were used but it was the submarines that were the main German threat.

At the beginning, Britain was short of escort ships and a high tally of shipping was lost. During 1941 the assistance of the still-neutral USA made a difference, with American ships patrolling the western Atlantic. Once America had joined the war officially in December 1941 the Germans attacked shipping near to America, causing large losses.

Eventually the Allies gained the upper hand. Through the use of ULTRA intelligence, convoys were diverted from U-boat patrol areas, and equipment was developed to find and destroy the submarines. In May 1943 the battle was won.

'HAPPY TIME'

German term for periods in winter 1940–41 and spring 1942 when they were highly successful in their attacks on Allied ships in the Atlantic.

WOLFPACKS

The Germans operated their submarines in 'wolfpacks', where they would form a line across the intended paths of convoys. Once convoys were sighted, the U-boats would infiltrate to carry out their attacks.

21

Number of merchant ships sunk out of the 30 in Allied Convoy SC7 in October 1940.

Asdic

Submarine detection equipment, fitted on the underside of a Royal Navy ship's hull. Although effective, it had its drawbacks: Asdic couldn't detect U-boats on the surface and wasn't as effective in rough seas.

Huff Duff

HF/DF (high-frequency direction finding) was equipment used by the Royal Navy to find U-boats by detecting radio transmissions.

Atlantic Gap

As shore-based aircraft were unable to cover the whole length of the convoy routes, there were gaps where U-boats could operate without fear of airborne attack. The gap was eventually closed by Allied aircraft carriers joining the convoys and Very Long Range aircraft such as Liberators, B-17s, Sunderlands and Catalinas.

146

Number of U-boats sunk by RAF Coastal Command's shore-based aircraft. These successes came at a price: 741 Coastal Command aircraft were lost in the battle.

757

Total number of U-boats destroyed in the battle.

CASUALTIES (DEATHS)

U-boat crewmen	25,870
Allied merchant seamen	30,000
Allied sailors and RAF aircrew	41,000

NUMBER OF ALLIED SHIPS SUNK BY U-BOATS

1939

September	41	November	21
October	27	December	25

1940

January	40	July	38
February	45	August	56
March	23	September	59
April	7	October	63
May	13	November	33
June	58	December	37

1941

January	21	May	58
February	39	June	61
March	41	July	22
April	43	August	23

September	53	November	13
October	32	December	26

1942

January	62	July	96
February	85	August	108
March	95	September	98
April	74	October	94
May	125	November	119
June	144	December	60

1943

January	37	July	46
February	63	August	16
March	108	September	20
April	56	October	20
May	50	November	14
June	20	December	13

1944

January	13	July	12
February	18	August	18
March	23	September	7
April	9	October	1
May	4	November	7
June	11	December	9

1945

January	11	February	15

March	13	May	3
April	13		

63 PER CENT
Fatality rate of U-boat crews.

'IRON COFFINS'
German submariners' term for their U-boats.

DARING RAIDS: RUHR DAMS (16–17 MAY)

The Ruhr dams were deemed an important target because of the impact their loss would have on Germany's industry. They were difficult to attack by conventional bombs but inventor and engineer Barnes Wallis devised a method using bombs which would skip over the surface of the water. A special RAF squadron was formed: 617, based at Scampton in Lincolnshire. On the night of the raid 19 specially converted Lancaster bombers flew at low-level towards their targets. Two dams were breached, the Mohne and Eder, but losses were high: eight Lancasters failed to return, and 53 crewmen died out of the 133 that took part. Around 1,600 German military and civilians and Allied prisoners died as a result of the floods.

60 FEET

The exact height each aircraft had to fly. Any higher and the bomb would risk breaking on impact. As altimeters were not accurate enough, height was measured by hanging two spotlights underneath the fuselage, aimed together at a single point.

232 MPH

Exact speed to be flown at moment of bomb release.

24

Age (at the time of the raid) of 617's squadron commander, Wing Commander Guy Gibson. For his actions in the raid, which included flying alongside other Lancasters to draw enemy fire, Gibson was awarded the Victoria Cross. He did not survive the war, being killed on a mission in 1944.

DECISIVE EVENTS: KURSK (5–13 JULY)

On the Eastern Front the Germans massed for a large offensive against the Soviet forces contained in a bulge that pushed into German-held territory around the city of Kursk. The salient was 120 miles wide and 75 miles deep. Hitler delayed the start-off date, in order to allow more tanks to be supplied, however this allowed the Soviets more time to strengthen their defences.

On 5 July, Operation Citadel began. The Germans found their assault was ineffective: the Soviet defences were too deep and too well defended and they knew the Germans' intentions. The Red Army troops were better trained than those at the beginning of the war and they fought tenaciously. German gains were made, albeit slowly, but their forces became exhausted. Supply issues were compounded by Soviet partisan activity.

FORCES

	Germany	Soviet Union
Soldiers	770,000	1,300,000*
Artillery guns	10,000	20,000
Tanks/self-propelled guns	2,400	3,400
Aircraft	1,800	2,100

(* The Soviets also held a reserve of around 500,000 troops.)

PROKHOROVKA

On 12 July, at Prokhorovka, the two sides fought what is regarded as one of the largest tank battles ever fought. The Germans had new Tiger and Panther tanks which combined heavy armour with long-range guns, but were prone to breaking down and were not in plentiful supply. The reliable T-34 made up two-thirds of the Soviets' armoured forces.

ANTI-TANK WARFARE

Soviet troops would attack tanks at close range with Molotov cocktails and magnetic mines. German tank crews would counter by stopping their tank on top of a trench and then, by turning vigorously on the spot, cause the inside walls to collapse on top of anyone underneath.

Tanks at Prokhorovka

	German	Soviet
At start of battle	495	805
Losses	149	412

Although the Soviets lost more, the Germans couldn't afford to sustain such losses for much longer. On 13 July, Hitler called off the offensive. He had been apprehensive, saying the thought of the forthcoming battle turned his stomach. A few days before, the Allies had landed at Sicily and he wished to divert some of his forces.

Counteroffensive

On 12 July the Soviets launched the first of two counteroffensive operations:

Kutuzov, 12 July

Against the Germans at the north of the Kursk salient.

Rumyantsev, 3 August

In the south, the city of Kharkiv was taken at the end of August as the Soviets pushed the Germans towards the River Dnieper.

Despite heavy Soviet losses – around 850,000 casualties – the initiative on the Eastern Front was now in their hands.

BATTLE OF THE PIPS

This incident, which took place near the Aleutian Islands – a string of islands reaching 1,000 miles into the northern Pacific from Alaska – in July 1943, saw US ships attacking radar-detected targets thought to be Japanese ships. When no ships or signs of damage were found there was confusion as to what they had fired at. The official US Navy explanation was that the radar had detected distant mountains, but other theories speculated it was migrating seabirds.

PRISONERS

The Japanese idea about being taken prisoner is different from that in Europe and America. In Japan it is regarded as a disgrace.
Hideki Tojo, Japanese Prime Minister

The Japanese looked contemptuously at the Allied servicemen they captured. They were not expected to be captured and therefore thought little of their opponents who were. Prisoners were treated badly, being beaten, starved, overworked, and left to suffer illness and disease with meagre medical resources provided. Many were simply killed: shot or beheaded and in some extreme cases subjected to medical experiments. One crew of a downed American B-29 bomber died during vivisection operations. Other prisoners were used in live hand grenade tests.

(Non-Soviet Union) Allied prisoners death rate

Held by Japanese   27 per cent
Held by Germany/Italy   4 per cent

The Death Railway

In October 1943, work finished on the Thailand–Burma Railway. It had begun in June 1942. Alongside 240,000 Asian labourers, 64,000 Allied prisoners of war had been forced into working on the railway's construction, which was designed to supply the Japanese in Burma. Allied air raids destroyed parts of the railway, including the bridge over the River Kwai.

258

Length in miles of the railway.

77

Number of days Captain William Drower spent in solitary confinement, in a tiny cage underground. He was only saved by the camp's liberation, and emerged from his incarceration in a delirious state.

12,000

Number of Allied prisoners of war who died in the railway's construction. Ninety thousand Burmese, Malayan, Indonesian and Thai conscripted workers also died. Many of those working on the construction of the railway were killed by Allied bombing raids.

THE HOLOCAUST

*How can you bring yourself to kill such beautiful,
darling children? Have you no heart at all?*
Unnamed Jewish mother to Auschwitz
camp commandant Rudolf Höss

The Holocaust is the name given to the planned elimination of Jews and other groups from German territory. Hitler outlined his hatred for the Jews in *Mein Kampf* and their victimisation was a major strand of Nazi ideology and practice.

When the Nazis gained power they first persecuted political opponents such as communists and trade union members. When Hitler's forces moved into Poland in 1939, and then the Soviet Union in 1941, death squads targeted Slavs and Jews. Executions took place via shooting or mobile gas vans using carbon monoxide. The Germans became concerned about the effect this mass killing was having on their troops and looked to find a more clinical solution. In the summer of 1941, experiments were carried out on prisoners in Auschwitz using Zyklon B – a hydrogen cyanide insecticide – to kill. Its use would be expanded.

GROUPS PERSECUTED BY THE NAZIS

Mentally ill patients	Jehovah's Witnesses
The physically disabled	Black people
Roma	Freemasons
Intellectuals	The homeless
Prisoners of war	Criminals
Communists	Prostitutes
Deaf and blind people	Alcoholics
Homosexuals	Trade union officials

IDENTIFICATION TRIANGLES

Prisoners had triangles sewn onto their uniforms to denote their classification:

Jews	yellow
Criminals	green
Political opponents	red
'Asocials' (Roma, tramps)	black/brown
Homosexuals	pink
Jehovah's Witnesses	purple

CONCENTRATION CAMPS

Concentration camps were one of the earliest elements of Nazi rule, used to incarcerate political opponents and others. The first camp was established in southern Germany at Dachau in March 1933. Most were used as labour camps. Later, extermination camps, where mass killings were carried out, were constructed.

20,000

Number of camps built.

21,000

Number who died from the 23,000 Roma sent to Auschwitz.

THE FINAL SOLUTION

The term given to the programme to eradicate all Jews from the Third Reich. Plans were made to transport them from all over German-held territory to the extermination camps.

SONDERKOMMANDO

At the death camps Jews were forced to take part in the physical removal of bodies from the gas chambers and take them to the crematoria. In October 1944 at Auschwitz-Birkenau, members of the Sonderkommando revolted, setting fire to crematoria and attacking the guards. All were subsequently killed. Other instances of resistance had taken place at Treblinka, Sobibór and Chełmno.

Be strong, have courage.

Last words of Róża Robota as she was about
to be hanged, following her participation in the
prisoners' revolt at Auschwitz-Birkenau

EXPERIMENTS

The Nazis carried out many unethical experiments on prisoners, subjecting them to hypothermia, drug testing, decompression tests, castration, or infecting them with fatal diseases. Experiments were done to provide information for military purposes, research to aid German industry and to provide evidence for the Nazis' theories on race.

'ANGEL OF DEATH'

Nickname of SS doctor Josef Mengele. Mengele was responsible for carrying out many of the experiments at Auschwitz. He evaded capture at the end of the war and spent the rest of his life in South America.

SLAVE LABOUR

Prisoners were used for slave labour for construction projects, munitions work and in other areas of German industry. They were worked to death in the 'Annihilation through Work' programme. One of the projects was the manufacture of the V2 rockets, the head of which – Wernher von Braun – avoided war crime prosecution and became part of the American space programme.

ŻYDOWSKA ORGANIZACJA BOJOWA (JEWISH COMBAT ORGANISATION)

Group that organised resistance to deportations from the Warsaw ghetto. An armed uprising began in April 1943 and held out for a month, but was eventually put down by German troops. Over 7,000 were killed immediately and the rest of the ghetto's inhabitants were sent to the camps.

KATYN

In early 1943 at Katyn, Germans came across mass graves, containing the bodies of over 4,000 Polish officers, each of whom had been shot through the head. It was just one of the sites at which around 22,000 Polish prisoners of war and other prisoners had been executed following the Soviet invasion of 1939. It wasn't until 1990 when the Soviet Union admitted they had been killed on Stalin's orders in 1940.

> *We don't need grave diggers, we need heavy equipment.*
> Soviet NKVD officer Dmitri Tokarev.
> Graves were dug 20 feet deep.

AUSCHWITZ-BIRKENAU

Arbeit Macht Frei

This phrase – translated as 'work makes you free' – was set in the gates at Auschwitz. Situated in Poland, Auschwitz-Birkenau was the biggest extermination camp used by the Nazis.

THE LITTLE RED HOUSE

Jews arriving by train at Auschwitz-Birkenau were subject to a selection process. The healthy men and women were kept for slave labour and the weaker – the old, the unfit and the very young – were selected to be killed immediately. They were taken to the Little Red House (or its companion the Little White House) situated away from the main camp and told they would be given a shower. Once inside they were gassed with Zyklon-B. These gas chambers were replaced by four larger ones in 1943.

75 PER CENT

Percentage of those arriving at Auschwitz-Birkenau in 1944 who were selected to be taken immediately to the gas chambers.

960,000

Number of Jews killed at Auschwitz-Birkenau, from a total of over 1.1 million murdered there by the Germans.

6,000
Number of prisoners killed in Auschwitz-Birkenau's gas chambers each day in 1944.

FINAL SOLUTION EXTERMINATION CENTRES

Camp	Numbers killed
Auschwitz-Birkenau	1,100,000
Treblinka	925,000
Bełżec	434,500
Sobibór	167,000
Chełmno	152,000
Majdanek	130,000

1944

Daring Raids: Amiens Prison (18 February)

*Leading three aircraft to attack eastern wall
using main road as lead in. Second section of
three aircraft when 10 miles from target will
break away to the right at sufficient height to
allow them to watch leading three aircraft and
then attack northern wall on a North-South
run, immediately following the explosion of the
bombs of the leading section.*

These were the instructions for the first-wave
attack of RAF Mosquito bombers in their low-
level bombing raid on Amiens prison. The mission
aimed to create an opportunity for French
resistance prisoners to escape. Although some
were killed in the attack, around 250 prisoners
managed to get away.

THE GREAT ESCAPE

A quarter of a million Allied prisoners of war were held in German and Italian camps. Most were kept in rudimentary camps such as Stalag Luft III, near Zagan in Poland, from where in March 1944 the most ambitious escape attempt of the war took place.

A mass escape was planned, for which three tunnels were dug: Tom, Dick and Harry. Harry was chosen for 200 Allied airmen to make their escape.

365 FEET
Length of tunnel Harry. It was dug at a depth of 25 feet.

PENGUINS
Name for prisoners who helped distribute the dug-out sand around the camp. They kept it in bags hidden inside their trousers and would shake it out gently on to the ground.

EQUIPMENT
The tunnels required large amounts of equipment for the excavation, shoring up of tunnel walls, ventilation shafts and so on:

4,000 bed boards
1,400 milk tins
90 bunk beds

52 tables
34 chairs

Over 1,600 blankets were also used in the escape, for making civilian clothes, dampening the sound of the tunnels' construction and for the escapees to keep warm when out of the camp.

3

Number of successful escapees from the 76 that got out of the camp. Two Norwegians made 'home runs' to neutral Sweden and one Dutchman reached Spain. Hitler had originally ordered all captured escapees to be executed but was persuaded to allow some to live. In the end, 50 were shot.

DECISIVE EVENTS: IMPHAL AND KOHIMA (7 MARCH–18 JULY)

The Japanese 15th Army attempted to prevent a British offensive in Burma by launching their own attack into India. The objective was to cut the Imphal to Dimapur road at the town of Kohima, take the supplies at Imphal and Dimapur, and capture Allied airbases in Assam. The operation was named U-Go. In the face of determined fighting the Japanese were unable to achieve their objectives and without the supplies they hoped to gain, were forced to retreat. The heavy defeat – casualties were over 60 per cent – was followed by an Allied advance into Burma that saw Mandalay taken in March and Rangoon in May 1945.

'SAMURAI SHAKES'

Japanese term for visible signs of combat stress.

CASUALTIES

Japanese   53,000
British   16,500

KOHIMA

Fifteen thousand Japanese launched attacks on 2,500 British troops at the hillside town of Kohima. In early April the town was surrounded in some of the fiercest fighting of the war. The area commissioner's tennis courts became the location for close-quarter and prolonged fighting until eventually the Japanese withdrew following the arrival of British reinforcements.

THE KOHIMA EPITAPH

When you go home
Tell them of us and say
For your tomorrow
We gave our today

This short verse is inscribed on the Kohima war memorial and was inspired by lines written during the First World War by John Maxwell Edmonds.

106,000

Number of Japanese killed or wounded in Burma by the end of the war.

130,000

Number of wounded Allied personnel airlifted out by the RAF. Air power was crucial with supplies and troops being carried in to combat areas that would be next to impossible to supply by land.

'THE HUMP'

Allied aircraft from India airlifted supplies to China by flying over 'the Hump' of the Himalayas.

71,000

Tons of supplies flown into China in one month, July 1945.

> MERRILL'S MARAUDERS
> The only US infantry unit to operate on the Asian
> continent.

OPERATION ICHI-GO

In April 1944 over 500,000 Japanese troops began an
offensive in China, its aim to capture US airfields which
posed a threat to the Japanese home islands. Chinese
Nationalist troops were powerless to halt what was Japan's
biggest land assault of the war. Thirteen airfields were taken
and the Japanese linked up with their forces in Indo-China
where they fought Ho Chi Minh, who had helped the Allies.
The Nationalists suffered 300,000 casualties.

THE AMERICAN INVASION

Over-paid, over-sexed and over here.

This phrase was commonly applied to American servicemen who
arrived in Britain in advance of the Normandy landings. American
soldiers were paid five times as much as British soldiers.

A SHORT GUIDE TO GREAT BRITAIN

This 1942 booklet was issued to US servicemen to give
a thorough idea of British life and how they should
behave in the country. One section read:

The British are tough. Don't be misled by the British tendency to be soft-spoken and polite. If they need to be, they can be plenty tough. The English language didn't spread across the oceans and over the mountains and jungles and swamps of the world because these people were panty-waists.

NORTHERN IRELAND

US forces were based all over Britain. In Northern Ireland troops were stationed at 169 locations.

DISASTERS OF THE WAR: EXERCISE TIGER (28 APRIL)

A routine pre-invasion exercise on the Devon coast at Slapton Sands was taking place when German torpedo boats got close enough to attack. They hit three landing ships, killing 749 men.

DECISIVE EVENTS: NORMANDY LANDINGS (6 JUNE)

Okay, let's go.
US General Dwight D. Eisenhower on
the decision to proceed, 5 June

With the Soviets making gains from the east and American and British forces having advanced north after landing in Italy, an Allied campaign through north-west Europe was hoped to be the final element in the defeat of Germany. Operation Overlord was the western Allies' campaign to end the war.

Airborne troops would parachute in or land by glider during the night to secure key locations in advance of the main seaborne assault. Once troops were landed, they would form bridgeheads before reinforcements would assist the breakout.

1,700 MILES

The length of the Atlantic Wall, the defensive line running from Spain to Norway. The wall was a series of bunkers, gun emplacements, observation posts and anti-aircraft batteries, designed to repel any Allied invasion. Most of it was constructed by slave labour.

ARMY DIVISIONS (JUNE 1944)

	North-West Europe	Eastern Front
Allied	91	560
Germany	65	235

DECEPTIONS OF THE WAR: D-DAY

The Allies hoped to dupe the Germans into thinking the Normandy landings were not the main invasion. Fictitious army units were created in the south-east of England, supposedly poised to invade at Calais. US General George Patton was made commander of the fictitious First US Army Group, the Allied planners knowing such a high-profile figure would give credence to their ruse. Radio signals were recorded at actual army units and then broadcast as if from the fake units. The plan worked. The Germans refused to believe reports of the landings when they were taking place, convinced they were only diversionary.

As yet there is no immediate prospect of invasion.
German Field Marshal Gerd von Rundstedt, 5 June 1944

D-DAY, THE 5TH OF JUNE

The invasion was planned to take place on 5 June, but bad weather forced a one-day delay.

2,876,000
Number of Allied troops in Britain, in preparation for the invasion.

170 MILLION

Number of maps prepared for Allied personnel in the two years before the invasion.

ORDER OF THE DAY

Allied supreme commander General Eisenhower's order went to all Allied troops about to take part in the landings:

> Soldiers, sailors and airmen of the Allied Expeditionary Force! You are about to embark upon the Great Crusade, toward which we have striven these many months. The eyes of the world are upon you. The hopes and prayers of liberty loving people everywhere march with you. In company with our brave Allies and brothers-in-arms on other Fronts, you will bring about the destruction of the German war machine, the elimination of Nazi tyranny over the oppressed peoples of Europe, and security for ourselves in a free world.

6,939

Number of ships in invasion force that left for Normandy.

THE SPOUT

Area cleared in the English Channel minefield through which the assault ships passed.

195,700

Number of naval personnel involved in the landings.

200,200

Number of sorties flown by RAF and USAAF as part of the preparations before the invasion.

AIRCRAFT STRENGTH

German   890
Allied   11,590

'MARIE' AND 'GOUJON'

Pseudonyms of two French resistance fighters, Raymond Basset and André Jarrot, who, along with thousands of others, carried out sabotage and other attacks before the landings.

> *The Channel stopped you but not us.*
> *Now it's our turn.*
> Chalked message on British Horsa glider
> by British troops before taking off

23,400

Number of Allied airborne troops who landed by parachute or glider.

'ROMMEL'S ASPARAGUS'

Nickname for stakes placed in potential landing sites.

50 YARDS

Distance lead glider of British airborne assault landed from its objective, a bridge over the Caen Canal. Men of the Oxfordshire and Buckinghamshire Light Infantry, led by Major John Howard, secured the bridge and held it until they were relieved. The bridge was named Pegasus Bridge after the airborne troops' emblem.

LANDING BEACHES

Sector	British/Canadian			American	
Area	Gold	Juno	Sword	Utah	Omaha
Landing beach code names:	Item Jig King	Love Mike Nan	Oboe Peter Queen Roger	Tare Uncle	Charlie Dog Easy Fox
Number of troops landed on D-Day	24,970	21,400	28,845	23,250	34,250
Totals			75,215		57,500

156,415

Number of troops who landed in France as part of the initial invasion force.

258

Number of landing craft lost in the British sectors. Sappers – soldiers tasked with engineering and other non-combat battlefield roles – were unable to clear all obstacles and mines in time and much of the German artillery was still in operation.

HOBART'S FUNNIES

British General Percy Hobart devised unusually modified tanks with specific purposes for dealing with the various obstacles:

Crab	Cleared minefields by flailing lengths of chains
Crocodile	Flame-thrower
Bobbin	Laid rolls of matting on soft sand to form a track to allow the movement of heavy armoured vehicles
DD	Amphibious 'Duplex Drive' tanks fitted with propellers and canvas screens to 'swim' towards shore

THE LANDINGS

There are two kinds of people who are staying on this beach: those who are dead and those who are going to die – now let's get the hell out of here.
Colonel George A. Taylor, Omaha beach

The troops met with varying levels of success.

Utah   The least problematic of all the sectors as currents took the landing craft to a less-defended sector.

Omaha   The beaches were defended from raised positions and inaccurate bombing left most of the fortified positions intact. Assault was almost called off but close-in bombardment by warships and determined action by troops on the beach eventually broke through the defences.

Juno   The Canadians suffered heavy casualties at first but advanced the furthest inland.

Gold   Faced initial heavy resistance, but bombardment from the air and sea coupled with Hobart's Funnies cleared the way.

Sword   Lightly defended but the advance slowed as Germans mounted an armoured counter-attack that reached the beach in the evening before being halted.

27

Number that foundered out of the 32 DD Sherman tanks that set off for Omaha. Escape was difficult for tank crews and many drowned.

THE GRAND ASSAULT

> *The grand assault on Hitler's European fortress has begun.*
> *The Scotsman*, 7 June 1944

875,000

Number of Allied personnel in Normandy by the end of June.

ALLIED CASUALTIES (6–30 JUNE)

Britain/Canada	24,698
USA	37,034
Total	61,732

BREAKOUT

Once established on the beachhead, the Allies began to carry out their further objectives: the Americans moved westwards to take the Cherbourg peninsula, and the British and Canadian troops moved south towards Caen.

The 'bocage' (roads and fields on uneven terrain, encircled by thick hedgerows and woods) was ideal for defensive action and, coupled with effective German use of anti-tank weapons, progress was slow. The British were criticised by American commanders for not moving quickly to secure Caen, but Montgomery was well aware British reserves over the Channel were not as plentiful as those arriving from America. Eventually the Americans cut off the Cotentin Peninsula, secured Cherbourg and broke out to the west and south before turning north towards Argentan.

32,000 YARDS

The distance the Royal Navy ship HMS *Rodney* fired its 16-inch guns to hit German tanks in the assault on Caen. The city was taken in mid-July.

OPERATION GOODWOOD

Goodwood saw the British attack German positions south of Caen, towards Falaise. The intense bombardment allowed quick progress but the advance slowed as the Germans recovered. Traffic jams also contributed and it was called off after three days. Whether it was an intended breakout that failed – or a concerted effort to draw in the German forces allowing the Americans to break out that succeeded – remains a source of debate.

650 TONS

Weight of bombs dropped in 10 minutes on German positions at Cagny.

4,500

Number of Allied aircraft that took part in the preparatory bombardment.

1,100

Number of tanks used by the British in Goodwood.

Battalion HQ surrounded. Long live the Führer.
Message from German battalion at Colombelles, 18 July 1944

FALAISE

By mid-August the British/Canadian advance formed the northern part of a pincer with the Americans forming the other half from the south. They neared Falaise but did not close the encirclement. German resistance slowed progress and there were fears the converging forces would fire on each other. The gap wasn't closed until 21 August, allowing many Germans to escape, however those trapped in the Falaise Pocket were subjected to intense artillery and aerial bombardment. It is estimated 10,000–15,000 died in the carnage.

50,000

Number of German prisoners taken at Falaise.

40,000

Number of German troops who escaped the encirclement.

CAB RANK

A system whereby RAF Typhoon ground-attack aircraft would circle, before being called down by infantry units to tackle enemy positions or vehicles.

'HOLY ROLLERS'

In order to provide armoured protection for troops being taken forward into battle, the tank-like M7 Priest self-propelled guns were stripped of their guns. They were nicknamed 'unfrocked priests' or 'holy rollers'.

YELLOW ON YELLOW

Yellow flares were used by the British Army to indicate their position; Bomber Command used yellow as a target marker. When bombers attacked at Falaise they mistakenly bombed their own troops and as soldiers lit more flares, the worse the situation got. Four hundred casualties resulted, including 65 dead.

THE RETREAT

The Germans retreated rapidly across France with the Allies in pursuit, preventing them from forming a defensive line. By the end of August the Allies had crossed the River Seine and thoughts were turning to the war soon being over. However, the speed of the advance outstripped logistics and halts had to be called for fuel and other supplies to reach the forward units. The Germans made good use of this breathing space to prepare their next line of defence: the West Wall, which the Allies called the Siegfried Line.

450,000
German casualties (from 6 June to 21 August).

DECISIVE EVENTS: OPERATION BAGRATION (23 JUNE–29 AUGUST)

This massive Soviet offensive decimated Germany's Army Group Centre in Belorussia (Belarus). The German forces retreated in the face of a Soviet onslaught across a 700-mile-wide front. Minsk was taken on 3 July and Warsaw reached as the Red Army advanced 350 miles westwards. For the Germans it was a bigger defeat than Stalingrad.

	Troops at beginning of battle	Casualties
Soviet	1,670,000	770,000
German	700,000	400,000

300

By the end of August 1944 the Red Army was 300 miles from Germany.

TANKS (SEPTEMBER 1944)

German	1,437
Soviet	13,400

ILYUSHIN IL-2 SHTURMOVIK

Nicknamed 'Black Death' by German soldiers, the Il-2 ground-attack aircraft was a powerful asset for the Soviets, armed with cannon, machine guns and 1,300 pounds of bombs or rockets. It was strong, with steel armour protecting the two crew members. Over 36,000 were built.

DISASTERS OF THE WAR: WARSAW UPRISING (1 AUGUST–2 OCTOBER)

As the Germans departed, on 1 August the lightly armed underground Polish Home Army began its uprising to establish control of the city before the Soviets could enter the city. However, the Germans returned to put down the action and the Soviet forces didn't intervene as their enemy crushed the uprising and flattened the city.

'ONE BULLET, ONE GERMAN'

Posters bearing this message were distributed around the city by the Home Army.

200,000
Number of Poles who died, including 15,000 of the Home Army.

Valkyrie

Code name for plan by senior German officers to assassinate Hitler in order to end the war. German staff officer Claus von Stauffenberg was able to smuggle a bomb into Hitler's meeting room on 20 July 1944. The bomb exploded, and von Stauffenberg left for Berlin, not knowing his plan had failed: Hitler was still alive. Von Stauffenberg was shot and his fellow conspirators were tortured then executed. The executions were filmed and German officials and military personnel were invited to watch the subsequent film.

The Champagne Campaign

The decision to land Allied troops in the south of France to press the Germans from two sides was the subject of much discussion among Allied leaders – Churchill was against the operation as it took troops from the Italian campaign – but Eisenhower was adamant. The landings took place on 15 August 1944 and American and French divisions fought their way northwards, eventually meeting up with the rest of the Allied forces in northern France in September. As the fighting was seen as not being as fierce as that in the north, it was called the 'Champagne Campaign'.

THE BROAD FRONT

Montgomery and US General Patton each wanted to lead a narrow thrust into Germany, driving forwards to end the war sooner. Eisenhower, the man who ultimately decided the strategy, chose a 'broad front' approach which was safer, but slower and not one that would end the war in 1944. Montgomery would lead the northern part of the advance, driving north of the Ardennes to take the Ruhr area. The southern part would see the Americans under General Omar Bradley aim for the Saar area of Germany.

LOGISTICS

Supply lines were over-extended as the major channel ports were not all in use and one of the temporary Mulberry harbours in Normandy had been lost in a storm. In September the US Third Army had to halt as it had run out of fuel. As the Allies had damaged the railway system to prevent German usage, they now had to restore it. Road transportation routes carrying supplies landed at the channel ports were brought in to alleviate the problem:

Red Ball Express
White Ball Express
Green Diamond Express
Red Lion Express
Little Red Ball
ABC Haul

650 TONS

Daily average weight of supplies carried by the Red Lion Express.

714

Average round-trip mileage for Red Ball Express trucks.

75 PER CENT

Three quarters of the Red Ball Express drivers were African-American. US commanders didn't believe they were capable of combat duties.

ANTWERP

The port of Antwerp had been taken on 4 September but the territory covering the approach was still in German hands and supply ships were unable to get through. When the Allies took the city they captured 5,000 prisoners. With no other option available they were kept in the city's zoo.

68,000

Number of German prisoners of war taken by Canadian troops as they advanced along the northern coast of France capturing Channel ports. The Canadians lost 3,000 men.

THE STOMACH DIVISION

Germany's 70th Infantry Division was a collection of soldiers with various gastric ailments who were grouped together as it was easier to feed them the special diets they required. These troops were stationed on Walcheren, an island which guarded the Scheldt River route to the port of Antwerp. An Allied amphibious assault took Walcheren in November 1944.

FIRST IN GERMANY

On 11 September the first Allied troops walked on German soil. A small party of US troops crossed the River Our, on the border with Luxembourg and Germany. After claiming their place in history, they quickly returned.

SIEGFRIED LINE

The Siegfried Line was a series of German fortifications running from the Swiss border to the southern part of the Netherlands. Although the defenders were hastily recruited, and included old, young and disabled men, they put up spirited resistance when the Allies attacked in September.

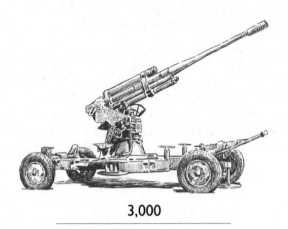

3,000

Number of observation posts, pillboxes and bunkers along the Siegfried Line.

20 TO 1

In September, the Allies had overwhelming superiority in tank numbers.

BATTLE OF HÜRTGEN FOREST

As part of the offensive against the Siegfried Line, US forces battled to gain three woods, one of which was at Hürtgen. Starting in September it descended into a bloody battle lasting several months, where the Americans suffered over 33,000 casualties.

DISASTERS OF THE WAR: ARNHEM

Sir, I think we might be going a bridge too far.
Lieutenant General Frederick Browning to
Field Marshal Bernard Montgomery

Operation Market Garden was a bold plan by the normally careful Montgomery to secure river and canal crossings in the eastern part of the Netherlands and obtain a crossing over the Lower Rhine. Allied airborne troops would hold the bridges while British Army tanks and men would force their way north to relieve them. The first landings took place on 17 September 1944.

Army Units	Objectives
US 101st Airborne Division	Eindhoven, Zon, Veghel
US 82nd Airborne Division	Nijmegen, Grave
British 1st Airborne Division	Arnhem

9TH AND 10TH SS PANZER DIVISIONS

These two divisions were sent to Arnhem to recuperate after fighting in Normandy. Their presence was discovered before the operation by British codebreakers but the information was not acted upon.

64 MILES

Distance to Arnhem bridge from starting point of the British tank advance. Units of the British Second Army were tasked with the push north but their progress went behind schedule as they faced solid German resistance, which had damaged or destroyed bridges. Another impediment to rapid progress was having to move all men and vehicles up a single road.

19,000

Number of airborne troops landed on first day.

ARNHEM BRIDGE

The British paratroopers had to fight their way into the town and then to the bridge. The northern end of the crossing was secured but not the southern part, which remained in German hands throughout.

8 MILES

Distance the landing sites were from Arnhem road bridge.

600–700

Number of troops who reached Arnhem bridge, from the 6,000 who landed. They held out for four days but resupply drops fell into German hands and under heavy bombardment and infantry attacks the paratroopers were forced out of their positions.

Essential every effort is made to ensure earliest arrival Guards Division at Arnhem. Situation at bridge critical.

Message from 1st Airborne Division,
Wednesday 20 September 1944

NIJMEGEN

At Nijmegen, south of Arnhem, renewed US and British attacks were made. Canvas boats were used by the 82nd Airborne's paratroopers to cross the River Waal. Heavy casualties resulted. The British tanks charged across the road bridge and linked up with the Americans. The armoured convoy continued north but was unable to reach Arnhem in time.

OOSTERBEEK

The British soldiers were pushed back and formed a defensive position in the Oosterbeek suburb. They were evacuated over the river in small boats on the evening of 25 September – after nine days of fighting.

13 DAYS

Length of time British officer Tony Deane-Drummond spent hiding in a tiny cupboard in an Arnhem house. The house was occupied by the Germans and Deane-Drummond survived on water, bread and lard. He escaped and was sheltered by Dutch civilians, including the family of future Hollywood actress Audrey Hepburn.

CASUALTIES – BRITISH 1ST AIRBORNE DIVISION

Killed:	1,300
Seriously injured:	1,700
POW:	4,500
Evacuated/escaped:	2,827
Total:	10,327

In the fighting to clear the way to Arnhem, the American paratroopers suffered 3,542 casualties; the British Second Army 3,716. Figures are difficult to determine for the whole offensive but at Arnhem, German casualties amounted to 1,100 dead and 2,200 wounded.

French Resistance

With the imminent Allied invasion in mind, acts of sabotage by French civilians in factories were coupled with ambushes and train derailments, assassinations and other actions. Groups of armed resistance fighters (the Maquis) lived in woods and mountain areas where they were difficult to track down. The Germans retaliated against resistance attacks, causing great loss of life in French towns through reprisal shootings.

Town/village	Number killed	Date
Ascq	86	April 1944
Tulle	213	June 1944
Oradour-sur-Glane	642	June 1944
Maillé	124	August 1944

75,000

Number of captured French resistance fighters who died in concentration camps.

Battle of the Bulge

At 5.30 a.m. on 16 December 1944 German bombardment began in the Ardennes forest. It was a preliminary barrage to an offensive designed to cut through Allied lines to reach Antwerp, forcing the Allies to sue for peace.

The Germans faced thinly spread US troops who were inexperienced or recuperating. Bad weather prevented Allied aircraft operating – there was no aerial reconnaissance undertaken and the Germans achieved total surprise.

Although held up in places by spirited American resistance they were able to force their way towards the river Meuse. The Allies rallied as the Germans ran into fuel shortages and when the weather improved the ground-attack forces were able to operate effectively. The subsequent counter-attack retook all the lost ground by the end of January 1945.

GERMAN ASSAULT FORCES

275,000 troops
2,000 artillery guns and rocket launchers
2,600 armoured vehicles

The Germans had a three-to-one advantage in infantry numbers.

Nuts.

US Brigadier General Anthony C. McAuliffe's response to being asked to surrender at Bastogne. McAuliffe was the garrison commander of the town, which was completely surrounded by 21 December. Patton orchestrated a rapid redeployment of his troops who broke through and relieved the garrison after they had held out for 10 days.

CASUALTIES OF THE BATTLE

Allied: 77,000   German: 92,000

PACIFIC WAR

Whether we attack, or whether we stay where we are, there is only death.

Japanese Lieutenant General Yoshitsuga Saito, Saipan.
Saito killed himself at the end of the battle.

Following Guadalcanal, US commanders considered two options: attacking towards the Philippines via New Guinea, or 'island hopping' through the central Pacific towards Japan. In March 1943 both routes were given the go-ahead. General Douglas MacArthur would lead in the south-west; Admiral Chester Nimitz would command the central Pacific forces.

THE CENTRAL PACIFIC ADVANCE

As the Americans moved from one set of islands to the next they encountered tough opposition. The Japanese fought to the bitter end, resulting in huge casualty rates. On Tarawa from a force of 4,836 only 17 were captured alive. One hundred per cent of the Japanese garrison of Apamama died, killing themselves before the Americans reached them.

Date of campaign	Islands attacked
1943	
November	Gilbert Islands: Tarawa, Makin, Apamama
1944	
January/February	Marshall Islands: Kwajalein, Majuro, Eniwetok

February	Caroline Islands: Truk
June/July/August	Marianas: Saipan, Tinian, Guam
September/October/November	Palau Islands: Angaur, Peleliu
1945	
February/March	Iwo Jima
April/May/June	Okinawa

USS *LISCOME BAY*

At the Gilbert Islands, the carrier USS *Liscome Bay* was hit by torpedoes. It exploded and parts of the ship and crew landed on the USS *New Mexico*, sailing a mile away.

DECISIVE EVENTS: BATTLE OF THE PHILIPPINE SEA/'GREAT MARIANAS TURKEY SHOOT' (19–20 JUNE)

When the US landed forces on Saipan, the Japanese responded and attacked the US invasion fleet. Nine Japanese aircraft carriers faced 15 American in the last carrier battle of the war. The Japanese pilots were less experienced and the Americans were able to dominate the aerial battle. In one raid, 73 Japanese aircraft were lost out of 82. The battle gained the name the 'Great Marianas Turkey Shoot', so heavy were the Japanese aerial losses.

JAPANESE FIGHTER/GROUND-ATTACK AIRCRAFT

Before the battle: 430
After: 35

LOSSES (AIRMEN)

Japanese 445
American 76

SAIPAN

Saipan was a vital objective for the Americans, as its airfields would allow B-29 heavy bombers to reach Japan. The Japanese defence was typically fiercely fought – in one battle the Japanese suffered four times the casualties of the Americans – but the US marines eventually prevailed.

MARPI POINT

The exploding grenades cut the mob into patches of dead, dying, and wounded, and for the first time we actually saw water that ran red with human blood.
Lieutenant Frederic A. Stott, US Marines

At Marpi Point on Saipan, hundreds of Japanese civilians jumped to their deaths from sea cliffs, rather than be captured by the US troops, who they had been told would kill them. Japanese troops also killed their own civilians. One five-year-old boy was saved when he was caught on a tree during his fall and survived the war.

天皇陛下萬歲 *(Long live the Emperor)*

Cry shouted by civilians as they jumped. Japanese troops also shouted this as they carried out final, desperate attacks on American positions, which were referred to as 'banzai' attacks. At Saipan, 4,311 Japanese were killed in this form of suicidal, frontal attack on 6 July at Tanapag Plain.

918

US dead from two battalions of the army's 105th Infantry Regiment, out of 1,100 men who faced a banzai attack at Tanapag.

LOSSES AT SAIPAN

Japanese: 23,811   US: 3,235

PELELIU

The two islands of Peleliu and Angaur in the Palau Islands were invaded in September 1944. On Peleliu the US Marines' 1st Regiment suffered the heaviest losses of any marines unit as Japanese resistance was carried out in typically determined fashion. The defenders saw less than 20 survive from the 11,000 stationed on the island.

SHORTEST MISSIONS

With the airfield captured on Peleliu, US planes were able to fly ground-attack missions to support their troops on the island. They would take off, attack, then land again to rearm with seconds. Pilots didn't bother retracting the undercarriage to save time.

46 °C

Temperature reached during the second day of the invasion on Peleliu. More men suffered from heat exhaustion than combat injuries.

ASIATIC

US marine term for period of melancholy and depression.

CODE TALKERS

Native American Navajo marines were used to send and receive messages that proved indecipherable to Japanese cryptoanalysts.

Invasion of the Philippines

I have returned.
General Douglas MacArthur, 20 October 1944

MacArthur had led his forces as they advanced along the Solomon Islands and New Guinea. By October 1944 they were now poised for the invasion of the Philippines, from where MacArthur had left in the face of Japanese invasion two years previously.

US troops began their invasion with the biggest amphibious landing of the Pacific War on the island of Leyte. Seven hundred ships formed part of the naval force.

In two months of fierce fighting, the Japanese garrison was finally defeated and the Americans moved on to the main island of Luzon, home of the capital Manila. The Japanese defended the city, causing widespread damage, exacerbated by artillery shelling from both sides. As many as 100,000 civilians were killed by the time Manila was taken in March 1945. Fighting in the Philippines was still ongoing when the war officially ended.

Leyte losses (deaths)

American: 3,500
Japanese: 49,000

Escuadrón Aéreo de Pelea 201

This unit of the Mexican Air Force, consisting of 36 pilots, took part in the Philippines campaign.

DECISIVE BATTLES: LEYTE GULF (23–25 OCTOBER)

In one of the largest ever sea battles, the US Navy faced the Imperial Japanese Navy in a complicated engagement. The Japanese attempted to thwart the US landings on Leyte with a strategy that involved three groups of warships. The battle raged for three days and resulted in the demise of the Japanese navy as a force capable of defending the home islands.

19

Number of US torpedoes that hit the Japanese battleship *Musashi*. With 17 bombs also hitting it, the giant warship was unable to survive. It capsized and sunk.

WARSHIPS LOST AT LEYTE GULF

US	6
Japanese	26

Do not plan for my return.

Letter sent in June 1944, from Japanese garrison commander General Tadamichi Kuribayashi to his wife.

Motoko.
I am taking on my plane the doll you liked so much after you were born. So you will be with me until the last moment. I just wanted you to know that you were with me. Dad

Last letter by kamikaze pilot Masahisa Uemura to his daughter. He died in a kamikaze attack on 26 October 1944

TIRPITZ RAIDS

Germany's largest ship of the war, the battleship *Tirpitz* was a major threat to shipping and its destruction was made a priority. Although it took part in a few operations its main contribution to the German war effort was in diverting Allied resources as they attempted to sink her as she sat berthed in Norway.

Date	Attack method	Result
1 November 1942	Royal Navy Chariot human torpedoes	No damage
22 September 1943	Royal Navy X-craft midget submarines	Extensive damage
3 April 1944	Royal Navy aircraft	Extensive damage
22 August 1944	Royal Navy aircraft	No damage
24 August 1944	Royal Navy aircraft	Slight damage
29 August 1944	Royal Navy aircraft	No damage
15 September 1944	RAF Lancasters with 12,000 lb 'Tallboy' bombs	Made unseaworthy
29 October 1944	RAF Lancasters with 12,000 lb 'Tallboy' bombs	No damage
12 November 1944	RAF Lancasters with 12,000 lb 'Tallboy' bombs	Capsized

Retaliation weapons: V1 and V2

Making a noise like a Model-T Ford going up a hill.
Royal Observer Corps description of the first V1 to attack Britain

There were two main *vergeltungswaffen* (retaliation weapons) used: the V1 flying bomb and the V2 ballistic rocket.

V1

World's first effective cruise missile. Launched from ramps or aircraft based in Europe. Once airborne they flew on set courses at low altitude, flying on autopilot until the target was reached, when the fuel supply was cut off and the bomb automatically dropped to its target.

Defence

V1s flew at low level and although fast, could be caught by skilful pilots. RAF Spitfires, Tempests, Typhoons and Mosquitos were used and had success in either shooting them down, or flying beside the flying bombs and tipping them over with their wings. Britain's first operational jet fighter, the Gloster Meteor, also took part. A third of V1s were brought down by fighters.

316

Number of V1s launched against Britain on the busiest day: 3 August.

107,000

Number of houses destroyed by V1s.

MANCHESTER

On Christmas Eve 1944, a V1 reached Manchester. It had been carried by a Heinkel He 111 bomber and air-launched over the North Sea.

59

Number of V1s downed by RAF pilot Squadron Leader Joe Berry of 501 Squadron.

V2

World's first long-range ballistic weapon, able to reach targets in Britain from its launch sites in north-west Europe. The V2 was impossible to shoot down as once it had reached its maximum altitude it descended at 2,500 miles an hour. The only effective counter measure was to bomb its manufacturing or launch facilities.

CHISWICK

The first V2 to reach Britain struck at Chiswick, on 8 September 1944, killing three people and injuring 10. News that Britain was under attack by long-range German rockets was not released until November.

168

Number of people killed in the worst British V2 attack, when a rocket hit a Woolworths store at New Cross Road in London on 25 November 1944. One hundred and twenty-three people were injured.

561

Number of civilians and military personnel killed when a V2 landed on a cinema in Antwerp on 16 December 1944.

COMPARISON

	V1	V2
Length (feet)	27	46
Weight (tons)	2.2	12.7
Warhead weight (lb)	1,875	1,650
Maximum speed (mph)	400	3,600
Operating altitude (feet)	2/3,000	315,000
Range (miles)	130	220
Number launched at Britain	10,492	1,403
Number hit British targets	2,419	1,115
Number launched against European targets	11,988	1,766
Powerplant	Pulse-jet	Rocket
First used	June 1944	September 1944
Casualties (killed)	6,184	2,754
Casualties (seriously wounded)	17,981	6,523

1945

After its successes in 1944, the Soviet Union marshalled its numerous forces for a large-scale offensive, to be launched from its positions on the Vistula River. Following a decimating artillery barrage, the Red Army advanced quickly westwards on multiple fronts. Warsaw was taken in three days and by the end of January the Red Army was close to Berlin. The Soviet advance on the German capital was paused as supply lines had become extended and a German counter-attack on Marshal Georgy Zhukov's forces resulted in the Soviets attacking north to protect their flank in March.

40 MILES

Distance from Berlin the Red Army reached as it halted at the River Oder.

It was an army of rapists.

Natalya Gesse, Soviet war correspondent, Germany 1945

As they advanced, Red Army troops attacked German women, raping an estimated 2 million. Soviet women who had been liberated from forced labour camps were also raped.

8.35 MILLION

Number of German refugees attempting to move away from the Soviet advance by February.

451,742

Number of German military fatalities in January 1945.

THE RHINELAND

The Germans' Ardennes offensive interrupted Allied plans and it wasn't until February 1945 that they were able to mount offensives in preparation for the crossing of the natural defence that was the River Rhine.

OFFENSIVES

VERITABLE (8 FEBRUARY)

Operation Veritable began with a heavy artillery bombardment of over 1,000 guns. The Siegfried Line was breached but British and Canadian soldiers encountered heavy resistance, especially in the Reichswald Forest. Eisenhower called it 'a bitter slugging match'. Bad weather prevented Allied air support and muddy roads delayed the movement of armoured vehicles.

1,600

Number of traffic control policemen needed to marshal the build-up of forces before Veritable.

GRENADE (23 FEBRUARY)

The US Ninth Army's attack was delayed by the German flooding of the countryside using water released from dams, but their push north-eastwards forced the Germans back and after heavy fighting Cologne was taken. Eight bridges over the Rhine were destroyed before American troops could reach them.

By 10 March the Rhineland operations were over as the Germans withdrew over the Rhine.

CASUALTIES

Allied: 22,800
German: 89,000

BRIDGE AT REMAGEN

On 7 March, after the Germans failed to destroy the Ludendorff Bridge at Remagen, American troops raced to seize this unexpected opportunity. The first man across was Sergeant Alexander Drabik who ran the length of the bridge under enemy fire. Eight thousand men were rushed across to secure the crossing – the Allies' first over the Rhine. V2 rockets were fired but failed to hit the bridge.

ALLIED AMPHIBIOUS VEHICLES

Amphibious vehicles were much in demand for carrying personnel and stores in flooded areas and crossing rivers.

Kangaroo	Armoured personnel carrier
Buffalo	Landing vehicle
Sea Serpent	Buffaloes equipped with flamethrowers
Duck (DUKW)	Cargo/personnel carrier
Terrapin	Armoured cargo/personnel carrier
Weasel	Light cargo/personnel carrier

DECISIVE EVENTS: CROSSING THE RHINE (23–24 MARCH)

On the night of 23/24 March, Operation Plunder, the offensive to cross the Rhine at Wesel, began as amphibious vehicles carried the first wave of attackers across. American and British airborne troops were then flown in as crossings were made in several places.

3,500
Number of artillery guns taking part in the opening bombardment.

118,000 TONS
Weight of supplies brought forward before offensive for the British Second Army.

2.5 HOURS
Time it took the airborne armada to pass a single point. Seventeen thousand troops were landed

from 1,500 aircraft and 1,300 gliders – the biggest ever single airborne operation. The landings were met with stiff resistance: 2,700 airborne troops became casualties.

INTO GERMANY

Montgomery had been given the task of leading the main Allied drive across northern Germany to Berlin but General Eisenhower changed his mind in March and the US Twelfth Army Group were given the prominent part of the advance, although not towards Berlin but to Leipzig and Dresden. It had been agreed that the Soviet Union would be the first to reach the German capital, a decision that did not please all Allied commanders.

BREAKOUT

The Allies broke out from their bridgeheads and pushed further into Germany. Although they encountered spirited resistance, they had numerical superiority and faced many weakened German units.

FORCE STRENGTH (DIVISIONS) (MARCH 1945)

Allies: 94
Germany: 65 (many under strength)

317,000

Number of German soldiers taken prisoner in the 'Ruhr pocket', an encirclement at Lippstadt.

200 MILES

Distance the British Second Army advanced across northern Germany in a matter of weeks. They took 78,108 prisoners, at a cost of 7,665 casualties.

ARNHEM

On 14 April Canadian troops captured Arnhem – seven months after Market Garden had failed.

FIRST CONTACT

On 25 April Allied and Soviet troops met for the first time as a patrol from the US First Army encountered Soviet soldiers at Torgau, on the River Elbe.

BRAZILIAN EXPEDITIONARY FORCE (BEF)

In 1945, 25,000 Brazilian troops joined the Allied campaign in Italy.

THE FINAL ADVANCE

With resistance ebbing away, rapid advances could be made. American troops entered Austria and Czechoslovakia. The Soviets had reached Vienna and Prague, and there were concerns they might move into Denmark but British troops moved north to cut off this potential advance.

27 JANUARY 1945

On this day Auschwitz-Birkenau was liberated, by Soviet troops. The date was selected by the United Nations as the International Holocaust Memorial Day.

BERGEN-BELSEN

I am liberated but then my life is crushed.
Jeanette Kaufmann, 21 April 1945

Jeanette Kaufmann was in Bergen-Belsen concentration camp when it was liberated by British troops on 15 April. She had lost her parents, her sister, her husband and two sons. Her testimony helped convict the camps' guards.

British troops were confronted with a scene of abject horror. An army medical officer described seeing a pile of bodies about 80 yards long and 30 yards wide, with the dead piled four feet high. An estimated 60,000 prisoners were in the camp at the time of liberation but around 13,000 died afterwards, too ill or frail to survive.

BOMBING OFFENSIVE: GERMANY

DRESDEN

On the night of 13–14 February 1945, 796 RAF Lancasters dropped over 2,500 tons of bombs on the German city of Dresden. Twenty-five thousand were killed from the blasts and ensuing fires. The devastation coming so close to the inevitable end of the war caused controversy among the Allies at the time about what was regarded as terror bombing.

17,600

Number killed in German city of Pforzheim in February 1945.

22,000

Weight in pounds of the heaviest bomb in the war, the 'Grand Slam', which only Lancaster bombers could carry. The Bielefeld Viaduct was destroyed in a raid by 617 Squadron on 14 March 1945.

89 PER CENT

Amount of Würzburg destroyed in bombing raid on 16–17 March 1945; 5,000 people were killed.

BOMBING OFFENSIVE: JAPAN

I believe that the destruction of Japan's ability to wage war lies within the capability of this command.
USAAF General Curtis LeMay, April 1945

The US bombing offensive on Japan's home islands began with high-level inaccurate attacks before LeMay directed the aircraft to fly lower. Incendiary bombs were used which, against the wooden and paper structures of Japanese buildings, had a devastating effect. Later in the offensive the US was beginning to run out of targets.

It's burning, burning, burning.
Sergeant James Hash, B-29 bomber rear gunner, during the bombing on 10 March 1945 of Tokyo. Aircrews could feel the heat and smell the burning buildings, animals and humans.

1,665

Weight in tons of incendiary bombs dropped on Tokyo.

96,000

Estimated number of Japanese civilians killed in the 9–10 March raid.

150

Distance in miles the fires of Tokyo could be seen. Other cities bombed in the offensive included Osaka, Nagoya and Kobe.

B-29 Names

Following a custom that began in the First World War, aircrew members personalised their aircraft. B-29s that took part in the raid on Nagoya on 11–12 March 1945:

The Canuck
Fancy Detail
Three Feathers
20th Century Sweetheart
Mustn't Touch
Tail Wind
Supine Sue
The Baroness
The Janice E
Adam's Eve
The Ancient Mariner
Gravel Gertie
Devil's Delight
Georgia Ann
Old Ironsides
Fever from the South

Pride of the Yankees
Homing De-vice
Slick Dick
Ramblin' Roscoe
Sting Shift
Pacific Queen
Frisco Nannie
Ann Dee
Black Magic
There'll Always be a Christmas
Booze Hound
Hell's Belle
Mission to Albuquerque
Snapefort
Punchin' Judy
20th Century Limited

PACIFIC WAR

IWO JIMA

The island of Iwo Jima, 760 miles south-east of Tokyo, would provide a welcome haven for stricken US bombers returning from bombing operations over Japan. The invasion began with US marines landing on

19 February 1945. The operation was scheduled to be completed by the end of February, but by then only half the island was in US control. The battle ground on until the end of March.

THE FLAG

One of the most famous photographs of the war was taken when the US flag was raised on the highest point of the island, Mount Suribachi, on 23 February. Six men lifted the flag that could be seen from any point on the island:

Mike Strank	Killed on Iwo Jima
Harlon Block	Killed on Iwo Jima
Franklin Sousley	Killed on Iwo Jima
Ira Hayes	Died 1955
René Gagnon	Died 1979
John Bradley	Died 1994

'THE MEAT GRINDER'

US name for heavily defended Japanese positions.

LOSSES (FATALITIES)

US:	6,766
Japanese:	19,977

1,083

Number of Japanese prisoners taken.

Okinawa

The force that landed US troops at Okinawa on 1 April was the biggest of the whole Pacific campaign. The landings were unopposed and for the first few days the US troops advanced easily until they came up against fortified Japanese positions. The terrain also helped the defenders: steep hills and thick vegetation. Despite facing fierce defensive fighting from the Japanese, the American numerical superiority in men and machines eventually told and after 82 days the last battle of the war had ended in an American victory.

29,810,953

Rounds of rifle and machine-gun ammunition fired by US Army soldiers at Okinawa.

Yamato

The Japanese warship *Yamato* and its sister ship *Musashi* were the biggest battleships ever built. They weighted 72,000 tons when laden – 20,000 tons more than the *Tirpitz*.

Ten-Go

Suicidal operation by the remainder of the Japanese fleet, ordered to attack the US Navy. Two hundred and eighty American aircraft attacked and sank the *Yamato*, the cruiser *Yahagi* and four destroyers. The Japanese fleet was finished as an effective fighting force.

Kamikaze

At Okinawa the full force of kamikaze (meaning 'divine wind') attacks was experienced. These suicidal flights in which pilots deliberately aimed their aircraft at Allied ships caused concern among Allied commanders. At times the Allies faced 300 attacks a day; 1,900 Japanese pilots died.

402

Number of Allied ships sunk or severely damaged at Okinawa, they included:

Ships sunk

17 destroyers
9 landing craft

5 minesweepers
3 ammunition ships

Damaged beyond repair

5 fleet carriers
2 escort carriers
1 battleship
1 cruiser
37 destroyers

11 landing craft
4 minesweepers
4 transports
5 other vessels

THE SHIP THAT WOULD NOT DIE

In one day, 16 April, the destroyer USS *Laffey* was attacked by 22 kamikaze aircraft. Despite five hitting their target the warship remained afloat.

MILITARY LOSSES AT OKINAWA (DEATHS)

US: 12,281
Japanese: 110,071

24,000

Number of Japanese civilians who died on Okinawa.

Remember when diving into the enemy to shout at the top of your lungs: 'Hissatsu!' ['sink without fail']. At that moment all the cherry blossoms at Yasukuni Shrine in Tokyo will smile brightly at you.
Kamikaze instruction manual, published 1945

DECISIVE EVENTS: BATTLE FOR BERLIN (APRIL–MAY)

On 16 April, the Red Army launched their offensive to reach the German capital.

Marshal Zhukov expected to be given the honour of taking Berlin, but discovered Stalin had set him up in competition with Marshal Ivan Konev, commander of the 1st Ukrainian Front.

Zhukov's 1st Belorussian Front faced the Germans

who defended from the Seelow Heights. The initial attack was not a success, despite a massive artillery barrage. Searchlights were used to blind the defenders but instead they affected the attackers' vision and confusion ensued.

In the south, Marshal Konev's 1st Ukrainian Front was more successful. Without waiting for pontoon bridges to be built, tanks were ordered to drive across rivers to keep up the pace of the advance. Zhukov's forces eventually broke through after three days.

1,236,000

Number of artillery rounds fired on the first day of the offensive.

2.5 MILLION

Number of Soviet soldiers amassed before the offensive. They faced 1 million Germans, many of whom were teenagers or older men conscripted into uniform.

INSIDE BERLIN

On 21 April Berlin became within artillery range and shells soon began to fall. A few days later the city was encircled – done not only to prevent Germans escaping but also to stop the Americans and British from taking a prize the Soviets felt they deserved. Inside the city, some German civilians killed themselves before the Soviet troops arrived; an estimated 100,000 Berlin women were raped by Red Army soldiers with an estimated 10 per cent of these women subsequently killing themselves.

FLIGHT OF THE GOLDEN PHEASANTS

As the Soviet troops closed in on Berlin, high-ranking Germans fled the city, after disposing of their brightly decorated uniforms. Hermann Göring was stripped of his rank by Hitler after the Luftwaffe chief proposed taking command of the Reich. Heinrich Himmler, the leader of the SS, tried to negotiate with the Allies to set himself up as German leader but was captured and killed himself before facing trial.

GREENLAND, NORTH AFRICA, MADAGASCAR, TIBET, MANCHURIA

Hans Baur, Hitler's personal pilot, prepared plans to fly Hitler to any of these possible destinations if the Führer decided to leave Germany.

HITLER'S LAST DAYS

Hitler had retreated to an underground bunker built under the Reich Chancellery, where he issued orders that were not grounded in reality, ordering army units to conduct counter-attacks that were impossible. Rather than be captured, on 30 April he shot himself. His new bride Eva Braun took cyanide. Hitler had tested the poison on his pet dog Blondi beforehand.

HERO OF THE SOVIET UNION

Soviet troops were told that the first to fly the Red Flag from the Reichstag's roof would be awarded the Gold Star Medal, thereby becoming Heroes of the Soviet Union. At 10.50 p.m. on 30 April, troops who'd fought their way to the roof raised the flag in an iconic moment signalling the imminent end of the war in Europe.

70 PER CENT

Amount of Berlin's city centre destroyed in the final attacks. On 2 May the battle was over and the guns fell silent.

305,000

Casualties suffered by the Soviets in the final three weeks of the war. The Germans fought tenaciously as the Red Army closed in on Berlin, losing almost half a million as prisoners. Over 120,000 Berliners died.

GOEBBELS' CHILDREN

The Nazi propaganda minister Joseph Goebbels remained in the bunker after Hitler's death. He and his wife killed themselves, but beforehand they arranged for the poisoning by cyanide of their six children:

Helga (12), Hildegard (11), Helmut (9), Holdine (8), Hedwig (6), Heidrun (4).

THE END OF THE WAR IN EUROPE

That concludes the surrender.
Field Marshal Montgomery, Lüneburg Heath, 4 May 1945

There were three surrender ceremonies that ended the war in Europe.

Date	Location	Details
4 May	Lüneburg Heath	Germans surrendered in north-west Germany, Denmark and Holland to Montgomery.
7 May	Reims	General Alfred Jodl signed Germany's unconditional surrender.
9 May	Berlin	The Soviet Union insisted a surrender document be signed in Berlin to make clear the Germans were surrendering on all fronts.

HEADLINE NEWS

'Germany Quits'
The Montreal Daily Star

'Britain's Day of Rejoicing'
Daily Mirror

'This is VE-Day
Premier is to Broadcast at 3pm: Two Days' Holiday'
The Daily Sketch

'It's Over in Europe!'
New York Daily News

'The War in Europe is Ended!'
The New York Times

NORTH-WEST EUROPE CAMPAIGN – ALLIED LOSSES

From 6 June 1944 to 7 May 1945 almost 165,000 servicemen died:

USA	109,824	Canada	10,739
Britain	30,276	Other	1,528
France	12,587		

THE INVASION OF JAPAN

We call upon the government of Japan to proclaim now the unconditional surrender of all Japanese armed forces, and to provide proper and adequate assurances of their good faith in such action. The alternative for Japan is prompt and utter destruction.

Potsdam Declaration, 26 July 1945

With the war in Europe over, the Allies now turned all their attention to defeating Japan. Operation Downfall, the planned invasion of the Japanese home islands, was to be in two parts:

OPERATION OLYMPIC

The southern island of Kyushu would be attacked first in November 1945.

OPERATION CORONET

Landings would take place on Honshu in spring 1946.

KETSU-GO

The Japanese plan to defend Japan involved fighting to the death and causing huge American casualties that would force it to negotiate. Approved by the Emperor, civilians would help defend the homeland.

DECISIVE EVENTS: HIROSHIMA AND NAGASAKI (6 AND 9 AUGUST)

With great secrecy America had developed its own atomic bomb – a weapon with power beyond anything ever seen before. Two bombs were readied and the first was dropped on the Japanese city of Hiroshima early in the morning of 6 August. The city of Nagasaki was bombed three days later. With the declaration of war on Japan by the Soviet Union, the pressure on Japan's leaders to end the war was increased.

Target	Date	Aircraft name	Bomb name	TNT kiloton equivalent	Number killed by blast/initial fires
Hiroshima	6 August	Enola Gay	Little Boy	12.5	66,000
Nagasaki	9 August	Bocks Car	Fat Man	22	40,000

It is an atomic bomb. It is a harnessing of the basic power of the universe. The force from which the sun draws its power has been loosed against those who brought war to the Far East.

Statement by US President Harry S. Truman
released after Hiroshima bomb

SHADOWS

The radiated heat of the moment of explosion was of such a high temperature it changed the surface of granite, caused roof tiles to bubble and left 'shadows' on the ground of people who were incinerated by this intense heat.

NIJU HIBAKUSHA

Term used to refer to Japanese who survived both atomic bomb explosions.

665,000

Number of Japanese civilians killed by US bombers in the war up until atomic weapons were used.

SURRENDER CEREMONY

These proceedings are closed.
US General Douglas MacArthur, 2 September 1945

On 2 September 1945 Japan officially surrendered with the signing of the Instruments of Surrender. The ceremony, overseen by General MacArthur, took place on the USS *Missouri*, moored in Tokyo Bay. Witnessing were two Allied generals recently released from prisoner-of-war camps, who had both been involved in the surrender of their own forces in 1942: British General Arthur Percival at Singapore and US General Jonathan Wainwright in the Philippines.

Post-war

Operation Unthinkable

With Poland, along with other Eastern European countries, succumbing to Soviet control and US forces departing for the Pacific, Churchill was concerned about the opportunities presented to the Soviet Union. He ordered plans to be drawn up to instigate military action against the Red Army. The essential American support was not forthcoming and the plans were shelved.

The Iron Curtain

From Stettin in the Baltic to Trieste in the Adriatic an iron curtain has descended across the Continent.
Winston Churchill, 5 March 1946

The post-war years were dominated by the Cold War, where former Allies stood against each other across the

Iron Curtain and around the world. Despite outward appearances the capitalist America and Britain did not have a warm relationship with communist Soviet Union, and tensions that arose in the war continued into the post-war period. The Soviet Union was determined to ensure it was never invaded as it had been in the war and so constructed a buffer zone of the Eastern Bloc countries, such as Poland, Hungary and East Germany. Both sides increased their spending on arms to achieve superiority in military terms. Although incidents such as the Cuban Missile Crisis and the crushing of the Hungarian uprising in 1956 raised the 'heat' in this Cold War, full-scale conflict between the two sides was avoided.

3 MILLION

Number of Red Army soldiers, including prisoners of war, sent to the Gulag at the end of the war. Stalin's control of the Soviet Union and the countries now inside the Soviet bloc led to years of terror for millions of citizens.

WAR CRIMES

Surviving senior Nazi figures were put on trial at Nuremberg at an International Military Tribunal set up for the occasion for four crimes: Crimes against Peace, War Crimes, Crimes against Humanity and Conspiracy to carry out these crimes. Sentences of death by hanging were passed on 1 October 1946. Göring killed himself before his sentence could be carried out and Bormann was tried in absentia. Similar war crimes trials were held in Japan.

NAME	POSITION	SENTENCE
Hermann Göring	Luftwaffe Commander	Death
Martin Bormann	Nazi Party Chancellor	Death
Joachim von Ribbentrop	Foreign Minister	Death
Wilhelm Keitel	Head of armed forces	Death
Ernst Kaltenbrunner	Head of Reich security	Death
Alfred Rosenberg	Nazi ideologist	Death
Hans Frank	Governor-General of occupied Poland	Death
Wilhelm Frick	Reich Minister of the Interior	Death
Julius Streicher	Nazi propagandist	Death
Fritz Sauckel	Head of slave labour programme	Death
Alfred Jodl	Head of armed forces operations	Death
Arthur Seyss-Inquart	Commissioner of occupied Netherlands	Death
Rudolf Hess	Hitler's Deputy Führer	Life imprisonment

Walther Funk	Minister of Economics	Life imprisonment
Erich Raeder	Commander of German Navy	Life imprisonment
Karl Dönitz	Commander of German Navy	10 years imprisonment
Konstantin von Neurath	Diplomat	15 years imprisonment
Albert Speer	Minister for Armaments	20 years imprisonment
Baldur von Schirach	Head of Hitler Youth	20 years imprisonment

RICARDO KLEMENT

Ricardo Klement was a resident of Buenos Aires who was kidnapped by Israeli secret service agents in 1960. He was in fact Adolf Eichmann, who played a major role in implementing the Final Solution. He was taken to Israel where he was tried for war crimes, found guilty, then executed in 1962.

89 PER CENT

Percentage of SS personnel stationed at Auschwitz who were not prosecuted.

RUDOLF HESS

On 17 August 1987, Hitler's one-time deputy Rudolf Hess died, aged 93, after hanging himself. For 20 years he had been the only prisoner in Berlin's Spandau Prison after the release of other German war criminals.

END OF AN EMPIRE

Britain had been nearly bankrupted by the war and struggled economically in the post-war years. Its days as an imperial power were over, with India becoming independent in 1947 and further colonies being relinquished.

RATIONING

Rationing finally ended altogether in Britain on 4 July 1954.

Items	Date rationing ended
Bread, jam	1948
Clothes	1949
Fruit, chocolate biscuits	1950
Petrol	1950
Soap	1950
Tea	1952
Sugar, sweets, eggs	1953
Meat, butter, cheese	1954

THE LAST SOLDIER

In 1974 Japanese officer Hiroo Onoda surrendered. He had spent 29 years on the island of Lubang in the Philippines refusing to believe the war was over. He only gave up when his former commanding officer personally rescinded his orders. Thirty islanders had been killed by Onoda since the war's end.

The War in Facts and Figures

1 IN 4

A US army report found that in combat only one in four American soldiers fired their weapons.

50 PER CENT

German infantrymen inflicted casualties at a rate 50 per cent higher than their American or British counterparts.

52

The Royal Navy ended the war with 52 aircraft carriers; it began the war with six.

148

British civilians killed by cross-Channel artillery guns.

182

Recipients of the Victoria Cross.

352

Aircraft shot down by German fighter pilot Erich Hartmann, the highest ever total for an ace.

1,355

Air Raid Precaution members killed.

1,525

Royal Navy ships lost.

2,076

Duration in days of the war in Europe.

7,046

Allied servicemen in Europe who were shot down but evaded capture, or were captured but escaped, and returned to Britain via the underground networks.

20,000

Frenchwomen who had their heads shaved for alleged collaboration with German servicemen.

22,252

Number of German prisoners of war who chose to remain in Britain after the war's end.

22,789

Number of Spitfires built.

43,000

Number who volunteered for service in British armed forces from Republic of Ireland; 38,000 volunteered from Northern Ireland.

53,000

French civilians killed by bombing.

59,192

Conscientious objectors registered in Britain by 1945.

60,595

British civilians killed by German raids.

80,000

Aircraft on the inventory of the USAAF at its peak in 1944.

170,000

British children evacuated to USA and British Dominions.

270,139

British servicemen and women killed.

800,000

Women who served in the Red Army.

955,044

In tons, the amount of explosives dropped by
Bomber Command.

1,500,000

Civilians who died from aerial bombing throughout
the conflict across the world.

2,920,000

Troops in the British Army at the end of the war.

3.3 MILLION

Soviet prisoners who died in German captivity.

26 MILLION

Soviet civilians who died in the war.

TOP TANKS OF THE WAR

Country	Name	Date introduced	Weight (tons)	Speed (mph)	Number built	Main armament	Notes
Soviet Union	T-34	1940	26	34	54,500	76 mm/ 85 mm (T-34/85)	Most-produced tank of the war. Its wide tracks were designed to cope with snow and mud.
Germany	Panzer III	1935	24	25	5,644	50 mm	Main German tank between 1940 and 1941.
Germany	Panzer IV	1939	25	26	9,000	75 mm	Panzer IVs were the most-produced German tank. In use throughout the war.
Germany	Tiger I	1942	64	28	1,347	88 mm	The Tiger's armour was 120 mm thick in places. It had a 6:1 kill ratio – the number of Allied tanks it destroyed for each Tiger lost.

Country	Name	Date introduced	Weight (tons)	Speed (mph)	Number built	Main armament	Notes
Germany	Panzer V 'Panther'	1943	44	29	5,590	75 mm	One of the best tanks of the war – a match for most Allied tanks.
USA	Sherman M4	1942	31	26	49,234	75 mm/ 76 mm	Second most highly produced tank in the war. The Firefly version's 17-pounder gun greatly extended its range of fire.
Great Britain	Churchill	1942	39	16	Over 5,000	2-pounder/ 6-pounder/ 75 mm	Well armoured but was not armed with a powerful enough gun to effectively tackle the heavy German tanks.

51ST (HIGHLAND) DIVISION

The 51st (Highland) Division was one of 24 British Army infantry divisions that served overseas. It saw action in the following countries:

France and Belgium (1940)
Egypt
Libya
Tunisia
Sicily
France (1944)
Belgium (1944)
Netherlands
Germany

Of all the fine divisions that served under me in the war, none was finer than the Highland Division – none.
Field Marshal Bernard Montgomery

NICKNAMES OF BRITISH AND COMMONWEALTH GENERALS

Boy	Frederick Browning
Jumbo	Henry Maitland Wilson
Ming the Merciless	Leslie Morshead
Pip	George Roberts
Pug	Hastings Ismay
Rabbit	Arthur Percival
Strafer	William Gott
The Auk	Claude Auchinleck
Uncle Bill	William Slim
Windy	Richard Gale

POSTERS

Propaganda posters were printed throughout the war, advocating recruitment, safety warnings, or to raise funds.

BRITAIN

Women of Britain. Come into the factories.

Coughs and sneezes spread diseases. Trap the germs by using your handkerchief.

Switch off that light! Less light – more planes.

You're doing a fine job… carry on canal workers.

Is your journey really necessary?

Be like Dad – keep Mum! Careless talk costs lives.

Go through your wardrobe. Make-do and mend.

Up housewives and at 'em! Put out your paper – metal – bones. They make planes, guns, tanks, ships and ammunition.

Dig for victory. Grow your own vegetables.

Use Shanks' Pony. Walk when you can and ease the burden which war puts on transport.

USA

Remember Pearl Harbor. Purl Harder.

I want you for the US Army. Enlist now.

Let's finish the job! Urgent – experienced seamen needed!

Doing all you can, brother? Buy war bonds.

Man the Guns. Join the Navy

Longing won't bring him back sooner… Get a war job!

We can do it!

Keep 'em flying!

Save waste fats for explosives. Take them to your meat dealer.

Don't crow till it's over. The enemy is smashing production records, too. Keep pitching!

Do with less so they'll have enough! Rationing gives you your fair share.

She's a swell plane – give us more! More production.

Soviet Union

The Motherland calls!

Under the banner of Lenin – forward to victory!

More metal – more weapons!

For the Motherland. For Stalin!

Go West!

Fascism is a starvation! Fascism is a terror! Fascism is a war!

Greetings to the fighters against fascism.

I am waiting for you, soldier – the liberator!

Germany

Front and homeland: the guarantee of victory.

Adolf Hitler is victory!

The slogan for 1943: Unstoppably onward until final victory!

Dutchmen – for your honour and conscience! Rise up against Bolshevism. The Waffen-SS calls you!

German glossary

Blitzkrieg	lightning war
Einsatzgruppen	mobile killing squads
Fallschirmjäger	German paratroopers
Flottenstreitkrafte	High Seas Fleet
Flugzeugabwehrkanone	Air defence gun
Froschschwimmer	Navy frogman
Knickebein	radio navigation system

Kriegsmarine	German navy
Nebelwerfer	multi-barrelled mortar
Oberkommando des Heeres	German army high command
Offizierslager (Oflag)	prisoner-of-war camp for officers
Panzerkampfwagen	armoured vehicle/tank
Panzerknacker	'Tankcracker' Stuka
Schlüsselmaschine	cypher machine
Schnellboot	motor torpedo boat (E-boat)
Stammlager (Stalag)	prisoner-of-war camp for other ranks
Sturmgeschütz	assault gun
Sturzkampfgeschwader	dive-bombing wing
Terrorangriffe	air-raid terror attacks
Unterseeboot	submarine
Wehrmacht	Germany's armed forces

ALLIED OPERATION CODE NAMES

Chastise	Ruhr Dams mission
Crossbow	Offensive against V1 and V2 weapons
Dynamo	Evacuation from Dunkirk
Flipper	Mission to assassinate Rommel
Husky	Invasion of Sicily
Anthropoid	Mission to assassinate Reinhard Heydrich
Lightfoot	First phase at El Alamein

Supercharge	Second phase at El Alamein
Mincemeat	Deception plan before Sicily invasion
Modified Dracula	Amphibious assault on Rangoon

FÜHRER HQ

Hitler used several headquarters during the war.

HQ Name	Translation	Location
Werwolf	Werewolf	Vinnitsa, Ukraine
Wolfsschanze	Wolf's Lair	Rastenburg, East Prussia
Wolfsschlucht I	Wolf's Gorge	Brûly-de-Pesche, Belgium
Wolfsschlucht II	Wolf's Gorge	Margival, France
Felsennest	Rocky Nest	Bad Münstereifel, Germany
Adlerhorst	Eagle's Eyrie	Ziegenberg, Germany
Berghof	Mountain Yard	Berchtesgaden, Germany
Führerbunker	Leader's bunker	Berlin
Führersonderzug Amerika	Leader's special train	Various

OCCUPIED COUNTRIES

Countries occupied in full or partly by German forces, from these years until 1945:

Albania	1943	Latvia	1941
Austria	1938	Lithuania	1941
Belarus	1941	Luxembourg	1940
Belgium	1940	Netherlands	1940
Czechoslovakia	1939	Norway	1940
Denmark	1940	Poland	1939
Estonia	1941	Romania	1940
France	1940	Soviet Union	1941
Greece	1941	Ukraine	1941
Hungary	1944	Yugoslavia	1941
Italy	1943		

NEUTRAL EUROPEAN NATIONS

Ireland – Sweden – Switzerland – Spain – Portugal – Turkey

10 WOMEN OF THE WAR

IRMA GRESE

Called the 'Blond Beastess of Belsen', this SS camp guard was notorious for her cruel treatment of prisoners. She had lampshades made of the prisoners' skins. Grese was hanged for war crimes in 1945.

HANNA REITSCH

German test pilot who proposed Luftwaffe suicide units at the end of the war.

MRS MINIVER

Fictional character created by writer Joyce Anstruther (writing as Jan Struther) who, in sharing her thoughts on life in wartime Britain through articles and a bestselling book, influenced American views.

ANNE FRANK

Sent to Bergen-Belsen concentration camp after hiding in a secret annexe in Amsterdam for two years, she died just weeks before British forces reached the camp. Her diaries give a poignant account of life under threat of Nazi persecution.

LYUDMILA PAVLICHENKO

This Red Army sniper was credited with 309 kills – the highest of a woman sniper. She toured America and Britain in 1942 to raise support for a second front.

VERA LYNN

Known as the 'Forces' Sweetheart' for her songs such as 'We'll Meet Again' and 'The White Cliffs of Dover', and for her popular visits to service personnel stationed at home and abroad, including Burma in 1944.

CONSTANCE BABINGTON SMITH

British photographic interpreter who made the first sighting of Germany's V1 flying bombs in 1943 at the Peenemünde facility.

Violette Szabo

The Anglo-French Szabo joined SOE to avenge the death of her French husband who was killed at El Alamein. She parachuted into France but was captured and died in Ravensbrück concentration camp.

Lydia Litvyak

Soviet fighter ace, who shot down 12 German aircraft before being shot down in 1943.

Rosie the Riveter

Character representing women working in the American war industry. The name originated from a 1942 song and is possibly based on aircraft production line worker Rosalind Walter.

In exile

A number of governments-in-exile were set up in London, forced out of their own countries by invasion:

Belgium – Poland – Luxembourg – Norway – Netherlands – Yugoslavia – Greece – Czechoslovakia

THE DEAD

It is impossible to give an exact figure for those who died in the war but reasonable estimates put the figure at around 65 million, which include those killed by diseases and starvation as a result of the war as well as battle.

These countries lost over 100,000 of their citizens:

Country	Deaths
Austria	370,000
Britain	330,000
China	10 million
Czechoslovakia	340,000
East Indies	4 million
Finland	100,000
France	600,000
Germany	5.1 million
Greece	450,000
Hungary	430,000
Indo-China	2 million
India	3 million
Italy	500,000
Japan	3.2 million
Korea	400,000
Netherlands	210,000
Philippines	100,000
Poland	6.1 million
Romania	500,000
USA	400,000
USSR	26 million
Yugoslavia	1.7 million

In spite of everything I still believe that people are really good at heart.
Anne Frank, 1944

Bibliography

Aircraft of the Royal Air Force Since 1918, Seventh Revised Edition Thetford, Owen (Putnam & Company, 1979)

Alamein Bungay, Stephen (Aurum, 2002)

Armageddon: The Second World War Ponting, Clive (Sinclair-Stevenson, 1995)

Arnhem Harvey, A. D. (HMSO, 1968)

B-29s Over Japan, 1944–1945: A Group Commander's Diary Harris Jr, Samuel Russ (McFarland & Company, 2011)

Barbarossa: Hitler's Invasion of Russia 1941 Glantz, David M. (Tempus, 2001)

The Battle of Midway Symonds, Craig L. (Oxford University Press, 2011)

The Battle of the Atlantic Williams, Andrew (BBC Books, 2003)

Bomber Harris: His Life and Times Probert, Henry (MBI Publishing Company, 2006)

Bombers and Mash: The Domestic Front 1939–45 Minns, Raynes (Virago, 1999)

The Bombing War: Europe 1939–1945 Overy, Richard (Allen Lane, 2013)

The British Empire and the Second World War Jackson, Ashley (Hambledon Continuum, 2006)

Carrier Battles: Command Decision in Harm's Way Vaughn Smith, Douglas (Naval Institute Press, 2006)

Chambers Biographical Dictionary (Chambers Harrap Publishers Ltd, 2011)

Chambers Dictionary of World History (Chambers Harrap Publishers Ltd, 2005)

Chindit 1942–45 Moreman, T. R. (Osprey Publishing, 2009)

Clash of the Carriers: The True Story of the Marianas Turkey Shoot of World War II Tillman, Barrett (New American Library, 2005)

Codebreakers' Victory: How the Allied Cryptographers Won World War II Haufler, Hervie (E-rights/E-Reads, 2011)

The Coral Sea 1942 (Campaign) Stille, Mark and White, John (Osprey, 2009)

Dresden, Tuesday, February 13, 1945 Taylor, Frederick (Bloomsbury, 2005)

German tanks of World War II Hart, S. and Hart, R. (Spellmount, 1998)

Hitler's Mountain: The Führer, Obersalzberg and the American Occupation of Berchtesgaden Mitchell, Arthur (McFarland, 2007)

Hitler's Navy: The Ships, Men and Organisation of the Kriegsmarine, 1935–1945 Mallmann Showell, Jak P. (Seaforth, 2009)

The Holocaust: A New History Bergen, Doris (Tempus, 2008)

Il-2 Shturmovik Guards Units of World War 2 Rastrenin, Oleg (Osprey Publishing, 2008)

Inferno: The Devastation of Hamburg, 1943 Lowe, Keith (Penguin, 2008)

Japan 1945: From Operation Downfall to Hiroshima and Nagasaki Chun, Clayton K. S. (Osprey, 2008)

Kamikaze: Japan's Suicide Gods Axell, Albert and Kase, Hideaki (Pearson Education, 2002)

Kursk 1943: A Statistical Analysis Zetterling, Niklas and Frankson, Anders (Frank Cass Publishers, 2000)

Kursk: The Greatest Battle Clark, Lloyd (Headline Review, 2011)

Leningrad 1941–44: The Epic Siege Forczyk, Robert (Osprey, 2009)

The Longest Siege: Tobruk – The Battle that Saved North Africa Lyman, Robert (Pan, 2010)

Okinawa 1945: The last battle Rottman, Gordon (Osprey, 2002)

The Oxford Companion to Military History Holmes, Richard, Singleton, Charles and Jones, Dr Spencer (Oxford University Press, 2001)

The Oxford Companion to United States History Boyer, Paul S. (Oxford University Press, 2001)

The Oxford Companion to World War II edited by Dear, I. C. B. and Foot, M. R. D. (Oxford University Press, 2001)

Pacific Victory: Tarawa to Okinawa 1943–1945 Wright, Derrick (The History Press, 2013)

The Real Dad's Army: The Story of the Home Guard Longmate, Norman (Amberley, 2010)

The Second World War – A Complete History Gilbert, Martin (Phoenix, 2009)

The Second World War Beevor, Antony (Phoenix, 2013)

Secret Agent: The True Story of the Special Operations Executive Stafford, David (BBC, 2000)

Stalingrad Beevor, Antony (Penguin, 2007)

Strategic Air Offensive Against Germany, 1939–1945 Vol. 4 Webster, Charles and Frankland, Noble (HMSO, 1961)

Tora! Tora! Tora!: Pearl Harbor 1941 Stille, Mark (Osprey, 2011)

Victory in the West Volume 1: The Battle of Normandy
Ellis, L. F. with Allen G. R. G., Warhurst, A. E. and
Robb, Sir James (HMSO, 1962)

Victory in the West Volume 2: The defeat of Germany
Ellis, L. F., with Warhurst, A. E. (HMSO, 1968)

*Viking Panzers: The German 5th SS Tank Regiment in
the East in World War II* Klapdor, Ewald (Stackpole
Books, 2011)

War Against Japan Volume 5. The Surrender of Japan
Woodburn Kirby, S. (HMSO, 1969)

The War at Sea, 1939–1945 Vol. 3, The Offensive
Roskill, S. W. (HMSO, 1960)

Wartime: Britain 1939–1945 Gardiner, Juliet (Headline,
2004)

WEBSITES

Bletchley Park – www.bletchleypark.org.uk
Imperial War Museums – www.iwm.org.uk
National Archives – www.nationalarchives.gov.uk
National Museum of Computing – www.tnmoc.org
National Museum of the Royal Navy –
www.nmrn.org.uk
Royal Air Force – www.raf.mod.uk
The Telegraph – www.telegraph.co.uk
United States Holocaust Memorial Museum –
www.ushmm.org
US Naval History & Heritage Command –
www.history.navy.mil
Winston Churchill – www.winstonchurchill.org

Have you enjoyed this book?
If so, why not write a review on your favourite website?

If you're interested in finding out more about our
books, find us on Facebook at **Summersdale Publishers**
and follow us on Twitter at **@Summersdale**.

Thanks very much for buying this Summersdale book.

www.summersdale.com